TWO FATHERS ONE WAR

Cpl Melvin Pollock 16089799
Student Post
4th AAF
Las Vegas Nevada

309 BS

LAS VEGAS RANCH NEV.
DEC 8
3:30PM
1943

SC. 3 PAR
AFRD, COLUMBIA, S. C.
MISSING IN ACTION.
Advise sender of correct
military add

RETURN TO SENDER
VERIFIED
1ST BASE POST OFFICE

missing

J. L. Smith Capt. A.C.
337 Bomb Sq.
10 Feb 44

CONTROL SECTION

Columbia Air ... Directory Service

U.S. ARMY POSTAL SERVICE
587
FEB
12
1944
A.P.O.

CONTROL SECTION

TWO FATHERS ONE WAR

Marcia L Pollock Wysocky

A daughter's story of two very special men who not only contributed to my life, but to my freedom; each of which I hold dear. You were so different and yet your lives have been eternally intertwined...

ISBN: 0988809109
ISBN-13: 9780988809109
Library of Congress Control Number: 2013909900
CreateSpace Independent Publishing Platform
North Charleston, South Carolina
First Printing 2013
please visit my website: twofathersonewar.com

Cover design by Troy D. Allen

Allen Studios, Waukesha WI

DEDICATION

Mom and I

I dedicate my efforts to my mother, Lucille, the common thread of this story. Thanks Mom for being my Mom. You are the greatest. You allowed me to choose my own path and yet your gentle hand nudged me in the right direction when necessary. You have held me in your arms all of my life. Love you Mom.

TABLE OF CONTENTS

PREFACE

Who would have thought that a visit from an unknown cousin would transform your life and alter your path? It happened to me. Not that I have always been certain mind you which fork in the road was beckoning me, but this was one of those moments when you knew the direction you chose would consume you for all time. It was a good thing. A really good thing. It was time to revisit what I had always ignored. The loss of Melvin L. Pollock.

If it were at all possible, I would go back in time and pick up where I must have left off. Oh, not so I could look younger or invest more wisely, or maybe, well, not have backed my new car into a flat-bed trailer.

I'm talking about not finding my past while I was on my way to the future. I did, at one time, ask my grandmother family questions. That's where I left off. She has been gone over thirty years. But when a man who served in the Pacific with my father passed away not long ago less than a quarter of a mile away, it was the icing on the cake of regrets. How close I was to an education I would have paid any asking price for. And yet it would have been free. And there were so many others like him.

Here's my advice to you, my reader. Start with the oldest person in your family. Take a tape recorder and ask questions about their life. And when you think that it's enough, ask some more. I know what you are thinking. No time. Boring. Excuse after excuse. Trust me, if you are at all human, someday, even if it's thirty years from now, you are going to think, "Wow, she was right! This is great stuff!"

Remember me when that happens…

ACKNOWLEDGEMENTS

Linda and Rick, if you hadn't found the boxes, this story would never have been told.

To the men of the 345th Bomb Group that I have had the privilege of meeting at the last two reunions, thank you for sharing your stories and for listening to mine. You brought me closer to my father, Melvin.

Clarence, thank you for never throwing anything out. You have given the word 'treasure' a whole new meaning.

Anthony L. Rutgers, you have brought tears to my eyes more than once with your kindness.

Troy D. Allen, what can I say. You give a whole new meaning to kindness, generosity and newfound friendship. Besides being a very talented man. *I'm sorry* I may have made you a little crazy.

Lawrence J. Hickey: Author of "War Path Across the Pacific." Thank you for welcoming me into your home and taking the time to talk about Melvin and the 345th Bomb Group.

Adams Times Reporter, thank you for permission to use photos and articles from your archives.

To my family and friends, you are the best. Thank you for all of the wonderful advice I was given throughout my writing. You helped tremendously. Your support and encouragement was always the boost I needed to keep going.

Above all, to Robert J. Wysocky, my awesome husband for giving me the opportunity to spend hours and hours on this work. Without you, life would not be the same.

INTRODUCTION

I have never been one for history. It was the past. And it's not that I couldn't wait for the future. I knew it would get here sooner rather than later. In looking back, it did just that.

But history was dropped in my lap the day two dusty, dirty boxes were discovered in the shed at the old farmhouse. As I opened the lids, I was immediately thrown back in time. I was now in the 1940's and caught in the realms of WWII.

Before me was the life of a young man who had joined the Army Air Corps. He had reported to the Franklin Street Armory in Chicago Illinois on January 17, 1943. In one of the first letters to his father he tells him, 'spose you're plenty lonely now. But it's all for the best, Dad - I can see right now we're here to go to it and I'm standing on the threshold of something."

The old letters were a treasure to behold and had such a story to tell. Then I found the picture. As I looked into the familiar face staring back at me, the tears began. I held in my hands a picture of my father suddenly realizing that all of the letters that were addressed to 'Dad' and signed 'your best son ever,' had been written to my grandfather.

As the tears subsided, I now knew that before me were some of the answers to the questions I had never asked. In this day of e-mails and text messages being deleted at the push of a button, I was well aware of how fortunate I was.

My father was an Air Apache and fought the war in the Pacific with the 345th Bomb Group M. He had flown only twenty-four missions before his orders sent him for detached service 2500 miles from Luzon. He and a pilot and radioman had gone to train 'the new guys from the states.'

The letters revealed the passage of time. Or should I say the passage of youth. The change, even on paper was evident. In 1943, he seemed to think he was invincible but by 1945, reality had set in and he knew better. While he was waiting for the ship home, he wrote, "Boy, I often ask myself how come I made the grade when so many others didn't. Guess I'll always ask myself that."

On March 17, 1943, St. Patrick's Day, in Wilmette Illinois, another young man just 19 years of age, entered the Army. His life had not been easy, so he was probably better prepared than most for what was to come. Little did he know at the time that he would be part of one of the most incredibly famous battles of all times, The Ardennes Offensive, better known as, *The Battle of the Bulge.*

What these men endured for forty-one days should never be forgotten. Nor, should it ever be repeated. All of these years, a font of information has been sitting in front of me just waiting to tell his story. But whenever he was asked, he would say, "*not today.*" But our todays are coming to a close so I am going to ask all I can, beg for the answers and tell his story as it should be told. With love and respect for who he is and what he has meant to me.

From the Pacific Theater to the European Theater, each and every veteran from this war gave their all and have memories to share. And each and every day, their words are being silenced forever.

We must record history while we can, whether it is from their written words or their spoken words.

My father wrote, "Illusions are a lie, but I want them near me; hope is another, but I want it to walk before me always." As we journey into the past together, into this time of *love*, war and peace, and *love again*, we will find that no truer words were ever spoken…

AUTHOR'S NOTES

I have strong feelings about calling a parent by their first name. It is disrespectful. Nevertheless, in my writing, I have done so more often than not in the hopes of not confusing you, the reader, or myself for that matter. Nor will I ever refer to Clarence as my stepfather. He too, was my father.

Melvin's letters have been edited somewhat. It is not that I have changed his words, but rather deleted those that seemed insignificant to the telling of this story. You will notice also that his letters have not been changed to indicate what we consider today's proper, nor consistent, grammar and punctuation. His method of writing his letters have been left as is including his spelling. It is how his 'Gram' also wrote, ie; rite, nite.

As for Clarence, I apologize up front if I have not *written* the emotion that I witnessed as he told his part of this story, as effectively as I could have.

I KNOW I'VE KILLED

Clarence: "When it all started, I said it was war. You knew you were there for a purpose. To get shot at and that's what they were doing."

Melvin: "I sure hope it's for the best. But I often wonder. War is no good."

Clarence: "We found a fallen soldier who had been buried in the snow for three days. He was wounded and yet did not bleed to death because his blood was so cold it had actually coagulated."

Melvin: "They said over the radio that my radio man was killed instantly by a direct hit of a 40mm. I felt like crying."

Clarence: "We took a beating, really took a beating. When you're up there and you have a gun in your hands and you run out of shells, what chance do you have, ya' know?"

Melvin: "So now I know I've killed, but it doesn't bother me. They'd have killed us if they could have. That's the way it goes in war, I guess."

Clarence: "They planned to present the Fuehrer with Antwerp by Christmas. They found out it wasn't that easy. They never did get there, did they?"

Melvin: "The other night we heard the Japs had offered surrender on their own terms. The President will speak this A.M. at 11 o'clock. Maybe then we'll learn if it's all over or if we are to keep on fighting."

Through these words of my fathers and the stories that surround them, I was provided with an education that could not have been acquired from any textbook or classroom. They have given me the most powerful and meaningful history lesson imaginable.

Instead of sowing their wild oats in the taverns and dance halls of their small hometown, they were overseas tossing boyhood aside and becoming men in the harshest manner possible.

They fought for their lives and they prayed to go home. They dreamt about the past and hoped they would live to see the future.

On the battlefields of Europe, Clarence's ever-present thought was of a certain brunette who crept into his mind night and day. Would he be gone too long and would she meet someone else?

In the Pacific, Melvin flies each mission hoping it is not his last. His everyday thoughts are much different from those of Clarence. He is going to make up for lost time where women are concerned. The girl he was dating when he left home up and married someone else. That was fine with him, he had no plans whatsoever of getting married any time soon, and he had been telling her that all along.

What he did not expect, what he was totally unprepared for, was being knocked off his feet by the same brunette that gave Clarence a reason for living.

CITY VS. COUNTRY

My fathers were about as different as night and day. Opposites Lucille would say. She said Melvin was 'city' and Clarence was 'country.' I have always thought this was an interesting comparison on her part but actually quite true. Their childhoods were certainly very different.

Melvin was raised by loving and doting parents. At the age of fourteen, he was attending Isabel Van Ells School of Dance and at the annual recital, he danced to "Turkey in the Straw" among other songs.

Melvin (in the straw hat and tie)

My mother said Melvin was quite the dancer in later years but would not have danced the polka. That just was not like him. I guess the dancing he did at the school was enough country for him, thus maybe part of the 'city' analogy after all.

In March of 1934, Melvin received a *'Palmer Method of Rapid Legible Business Writing'* certificate. This learning experience and his talented and over-active mind made for some great reading material that he plunked out on his old Royal typewriter years later. (I have that old typewriter.)

At fourteen, Clarence was certainly not attending dance class. After completing his freshman year, he quit school to earn his own way. He had been orphaned at a young age and his caring, but steadfast grandmother raised him and his four siblings. I wish I would have known this wonderful woman. They say God does not give you more than you can bear, but He seemed a little determined where she was concerned. Yet she persevered. She did more than her best and set an example that spoke volumes.

Clarence as a freshman

Shortly before Melvin's enlistment, he too lost his mother. This left my grandfather a lonely and brokenhearted man who waited anxiously each day for a letter from his only son.

Melvin entered the Army Air Corps with a young man's dream of becoming a pilot. That dream was dashed by a doctor who claimed he had a slight astigmatism in his right eye. (An exam three months later proved otherwise.) In typical Melvin fashion, he wrote his father that he was surprised because he always thought he was 'a perfect specimen.' His sense of humor was obvious in many of his letters.

Melvin, Bob Grefe, Shorty Southern, Pepper Martin, Leo Steiner
and Perry Steen all left for the service in January of 1943

Clarence's brother Edmund wanted Clarence to join the Army Air Corps, however, Clarence was drafted and he said, "that's when you go where they tell you." For him, that meant the Army. It wasn't long and he found himself in Fort Jackson, South Carolina, a stone's throw from Columbia where Melvin was stationed two different times before going overseas.

Even if Melvin and Clarence's paths had ever crossed, they would not have known each other. The two men never met. They may have been opposites as Mom claims, but I grew up knowing that they were very loving and caring men, and that they both loved my mother deeply. Under the circumstances, it was perfect.

I always knew that Clarence was in Europe during the war but it wasn't something he ever talked about. It seemed to me that whenever WWII was mentioned, however, not by him, so too, was the Battle of the Bulge. I was aware that he fought in this oft-mentioned battle, but I certainly never paid any attention to the fact that he was on the front lines when the Germans attacked on December 16, 1944.

Now as Clarence's gravelly voice tells me about that morning so many years ago, emphysema has taken over and he now fights a battle that can't be won. As time went on, our talks lessened. His breathing became more difficult and he tired more easily. Moreover, I was well aware that the memories became too overwhelming at times for him to continue. Nevertheless, when the words would flow, I listened with unrelenting pride for this man I call Dad.

His stories were of the bitter cold and of having nothing more than leather shoes for their feet. He told of the lack of food and most of all, the lack of ammunition. He told of the lives lost and the sadness in his heart. "So many young guys," he would say, "just so many young guys."

I began taking him books to read about the battle and he would look at me and say, "No thank you, I don't want to dream about it anymore than I already do." Eventually after it sat next to him a while, he couldn't help himself. That's when he would tell me that he never knew where some of the units were until now. Until he read about it well over sixty-five years later, he had no idea. He also reminded me not to believe everything I read. Not everything is true. Two things were certain, however. Many did not return, and of those that did, the war seems to have followed them home.

As the number of missions increased for Melvin, he often wondered if he would continue to 'go the distance.' Of the four squadrons that made up the 345th Bomb Group, his had the best combat record but also the most casualties. The other squadrons called them 'The Bloody 500th.'

In one letter home after the war he writes, "Now that you won't worry any more, I'll tell you that 5 out of 8 in my tent were killed, including my radio man & tail gunner. There's Gadbois, Lenhart, & I okay. You didn't know the boys, so it's okay, but when you'd go out & someone wouldn't come back, it didn't set so good."

They are dying at an alarming rate now, just as they did then. Statistics vary as to how many WWII Veterans are leaving us each day. Some say one every ninety seconds. Imagine how many stories will never be told. So many times I hear how someone knew of someone who was 'there' and yet never asked even one question or thanked them for what they survived. It wasn't that long ago that I wouldn't have either, but I do not hesitate any longer. I walk up to strangers now especially if I see someone wearing a cap that says 'WWII Veteran.' I shake their hand and I thank them for their service. Their smile softens and as they thank me in return, I notice a little sparkle in their eye. I often wonder if it isn't the beginning of a tear because someone remembered.

I will be forever grateful for the chance I have had to listen to Clarence's words about the war. Melvin's are only on paper.

When Melvin arrived home, he agreed to a blind date and one look at the little brunette (yes, the same brunette) and he knew his bachelor days had come to an end. He and my mother were married on October 2, 1948 and slightly over two years later, had what Melvin considered the perfect little family, a boy and a girl.

When I showed the following picture of the four of us to Natalie, Melvin's cousin, I commented on how Lucille had such a big smile. She said, "Her! Look at him!"

On November 11, 1951, we celebrated my first birthday together and five days later he was gone. He was killed in a tragic accident. His obituary states his age at thirty years, nine months and twenty-six days.

All of those missions, all of his dreams, all he had to live for and he didn't 'go the distance' after all.

The four of us in March of 1951

SURVIVAL

I often wondered how my mother survived emotionally. However, over the years, it became obvious. She is a strong and determined woman. What a privilege to call her Mom.

As I have been documenting these memories, her comment to me quite often is that there better not be much about her in this book.

I try to only smile (and not giggle out loud) as I cross my fingers behind my back and say, "Nope. Sure enough isn't, Mom."

I thought it was her comment that was making it difficult for me to describe her to you, but such was not the case. The words are just hard to find when it comes to her, but I will try.

She is the glue that has always kept us together, our strength when needed, our guidance when necessary and our unconditional love at all times. She gave us our foundation and taught us what the simple rules of life should be. She smiled at our every accomplishment and she smiled when we accomplished nothing.

She vowed she would only see the good in people, even when the good was hard to find. She challenged herself to be the best mother-in-law ever. She has managed this very well. My husband hates mother-in-law jokes. Moreover, she makes no bones about the fact that when she leaves this earth, she will not be angry or bitter toward anyone or about anything. Period. And yet she wonders what anyone sees in her. She has said this more than once where Melvin was concerned. I should add humility to her equation.

Her memories of Melvin have become quite dim over the years. When I ask about him, she tells me that they had such a short time together and it was so long ago. Once in a great while, something might come to mind and she will share it with me, but not very often.

Over these past three years, I was given the chance to get to know him through his letters and visits with his cousin. Throughout this time, my feelings have become bittersweet. They say you cannot miss what you never had. He has been brought to life as much as possible and a feeling of what must be mourning sometimes gets the best of me.

It was to be expected. Eventually, it was bound to show up. And it's okay. I have to be content with the fact that the stories of both men have not been lost for all time and will now be passed on for generations to come. Their words should be a gentle reminder that freedom really is not free and should never be taken for granted. I think in this day and age, we do sometimes forget.

TIMES HAVE CHANGED

So many young men and women were a part of what we now call the greatest generation. From the front lines to the home front, sacrifices were made and memories, both good and bad, were firmly implanted in their minds. From food and gas rationing to telegrams bearing the worst possible news, they became a grateful and stronger people. They learned to live with bare necessities and never waste anything of value. And everything had value of some sort or another.

Clarence recollects his grandmother knitting socks each evening while she recited verses from the Bible. The needles never stopped as she mumbled Norwegian words that only she could understand. Many times, she was reusing the yarn from a pair with too many holes to mend.

In today's world, we are a take-out, throw out, and get out society. Family meals at home have been replaced with fast food and containers that are tossed after one use. We will end a marriage without giving it a fighting chance, discarding it as if it were an old shirt we no longer have a use for. Always looking for the 'more' that is not there.

When is the last time you picked up a newspaper and read about who motored to who's home or who is expected to return home after a family gathering where a good time was had by all?

Where are we going? And why are we going in such a hurry? What happened to smelling the roses? I don't know about you, but I fear for my children's children and beyond. We used to take care of our elderly and now we ship them to expensive nursing homes where the care is less than mediocre. Families can't get along and yet we expect peace among nations.

We all want better for our children but is it really what we are doing? Are we accomplishing that by buying them all of the latest in electronics or occupying their every waking moment because God forbid, we don't want them to be bored!

When we were little, we played Annie-I-Over, roamed the fields hiding from our farmer neighbor on his tractor and bounced on the slash tree. Ah, the slash tree. It was a tree that had fallen over just enough that if you jumped on the trunk, it went up and down and you could bounce as if you were flying! What a thrill it was.

We built wooden airplanes that we could swing in and hung them from the most perfect branch in the biggest most perfect tree on the south side of the house. We were kids being kids. Plain and simple. We occupied ourselves. No one had to keep us happy. We were happy. And we did it all on our own.

When I look back at the differences between then and now, I think the kids are actually being cheated. In order to appreciate the good times, I think they need to have some tough times, too.

I admit to being caught up in this rat race of a world myself, and hope to heed my own advice. Because I too, am always motoring somewhere and I believe my nostrils are clogged because I no longer smell the roses like I used to.

We need to slow it all down a little and learn to savor what we have and learn to enjoy life. I appreciate all that I have, just at a faster pace. Shame on me.

Sometimes I think if we would pay attention to the past, the future would take care of itself. We must learn once again to be responsible for our own family and ourselves. There were no free rides back then. It was hard work, sacrifice and pride.

I was in the 8th grade the day President Kennedy was shot. We sat in the back of our classroom with the radio on listening to the news only to hear that his wounds were fatal. I remember it all like it was only yesterday.

What I really remember the most about John F. Kennedy was his famous and wise words that we still hear to this day. "Ask not what your country can do for you; ask what you can do for your country." Enough said.

DILL PICKLE SANDWICHES

Lucille Elizabeth Mikoda made her debut into this world on November 1, 1925. Ironically enough, she was born in the old farmhouse where the now infamous boxes were found. More on that later.

When she was just a few months old, they moved to a farm about a mile down the road. Many a morning while living there, Lucille remembers their mother waking her and her sister Grace up early shouting, "Girls! Gotta' pick the peas!" Lucille said from where the barn sat, the garden was a quite a hike and through a little woods. Now she remembers that fondly. Back then, not so much.

There were always chores that had to be done. Each day when they would get home from school, they would make a sandwich of tomatoes and dill pickles before heading down to the bottomland to get the cows. Lucille does not know why they called it that, or why their cows were there as this was not even their land. It was on the opposite side of the road from the farm. I never knew they had cows. To this day, I have never eaten a tomato and dill pickle sandwich. I don't know that I ever will, either. But being as it would have been a garden ripe tomato and a dill pickle that Gram 'put up'; well, never say never.

Lucille said it was about the time that she turned 8 or 9 that they moved to Monroe Center for a few years. Someone had talked her dad into running a farm there. They took everything with them, including the cows, and their other farm sat empty while they were gone.

It was in Monroe Center that Lucille began playing the accordion and became pretty darn good at it. So when Grace picked up a guitar and started to strum, the 'Mikoda Girls' were born. It was also while living there that Lucille caught the eye of a young boy who tells me now that she was *the one* way back then already. For him, it was love at first sight. Lucille's teacher had brought all of the kids to the Dellwood School to play ball and that is when Clarence tells of the first time he ever saw her.

Lucille and Grace Mikoda 1930's

The Mikoda Girls were usually the talent at Allie's, a little tavern in Dellwood, Wisconsin, where Clarence lived. Apparently everyone went to hear them play, young and old alike.

'The girls' were quite the celebrities and were even on the local radio station performing for their listeners. It was not uncommon for an ad to be found in the small newspaper reminding everyone to tune in.

February 16, 1940
The Misses Grace and Lucille Mikoda of Quincy will sing and play over WLBL (Stevens Point) at 3:30 p.m. on Saturday, February 17th. These girls play the piano, accordion and guitar as well as vocal selections. Be sure to tune in and hear the local talent each Saturday at this same time.

Newspaper ad for the radio show

In 1939, all of the eighth graders, Lucille and Clarence included, had their picture taken at the fairgrounds in front of the old pavilion. Lucille was not looking forward to high school. The school was in town, and they lived in the country. With no real means of transportation to get there each day, it meant living with different families in order to attend. She was seriously home sick the entire time and yet she also worked in Illinois during the summer.

When Lucille was fifteen between her freshman and sophomore years, she baby-sat for a little boy in Chicago. The family lived right by the railroad tracks and when the train would go through, she would cry just wishing she were on it going home. When she told me this story, I thought of Hank Williams' old song, "I'm So Lonesome I Could Cry." Do you remember the words? I certainly do, and they haunt me to this day.

Her sister Grace worked at the sewing factory with their mother's sister Celia, and Grace was able to live with her and her husband.

When I asked Lucille why she didn't do the same, she said she couldn't sew (still really can't to this day) and was not old enough to work in a factory even if she could.

Lucille was a junior in high school when Pearl Harbor was bombed and President Roosevelt asked Congress to declare war on Japan. Life as it was once known all over America changed dramatically on that day that really has lived in infamy.

Young men were enlisting or being drafted each and every day leaving their loved ones home with prayers in their hearts and a dedicated desire to do whatever they could to keep the home fires burning until they returned victorious.

ONE ROOM SCHOOLHOUSE

When you are orphaned at the age of seven, childhood slips away and you learn early on to work hard, share what you have and most of all, survive. It was not surprising that when Clarence entered the army, not only was his character that of a well-disciplined young man, it was that of a good man.

He nor his grandmother were dealt a fair hand. Grandma Emma found herself widowed in 1916 while carrying her tenth child. Two of Emma's sons were still living at home in 1931 when Clarence and his four siblings went to live with her. She was also helping her daughter raise two children. She was responsible for feeding nine, ten including herself. Baking powder biscuits were an affordable and filling staple at many meals. So many in fact, that Clarence would rather not ever eat one again.

Every so often out of necessity, Emma would write a note in Norwegian for the kids to take to their neighbor. He would read the note, go out in back to dig up a jar, put money and his own note in the envelope and send it back. When Emma sold a chicken or eggs, or whatever, she would repeat the process. Only this time, she would pay him back so that she might 'borrow' again when needed.

The children attended a one-room schoolhouse and each morning, Clarence would arrive early to light the fire in the stove so the room would be warm before the others arrived. On his way inside, he would set his 22 single-shot rifle in the corner so he could hunt squirrels on the way home.

His freshman year was spent with his aunt and uncle in Illinois. He was now in a school where they had swimming pools and over 1400 students.

Because he had been visiting there for so many summers, he was accustomed to the change in lifestyle. That year he earned a varsity letter for baseball, but out of necessity, he quit school before the following fall.

For the next three years, he held a variety of jobs, and usually more than one at a time. A few months before he entered the army, he found himself and a couple of his friends working at Badger Ordnance Works making the ammunition for the war. At one time or another, most everyone worked at Badger.

Before the war, he had decided that when he returned, he was going to be a builder, and the war convinced him that he would be his own boss and no longer take orders from anyone.

He built beautiful homes for people in all walks of life through the course of his working years. There were doctors, lawyers, judges; even motels in the infamous tourist spot we call Wisconsin Dells.

His reputation as a businessman and quality builder would be the envy of all. There was a woman once who found an old bill after her husband passed away. It was for $520. She was quite certain it had never been paid. She found Clarence and expressed her concern that she still owed him. Well, Clarence, twenty years later, remembered that the bill had not been paid, but the thought of her wanting to set things straight touched his warm and loving heart. That and the fact that she looked like she needed the money worse than he ever would. He gave it back to her with a smile and sent her on her way. I will never forget that story. And so many others like it.

Of course, before his contracting legacy could begin, duty called. After Clarence was inducted at Wilmette, Illinois, in March of 1943, he mustered in at Fort Grant in Rockford, Illinois. He then boarded a train heading for Fort Jackson in Columbia, South Carolina, where the 106th Lion Division had been activated two days earlier.

He was turning the page on another chapter of his life and one that he never shared with anyone. Until now, that is.

He does not consider himself a hero for having gone to war. Maybe that is not why we will always think of him as one. Maybe the good deeds of his life are where the true meaning of hero comes from.

STANDING ON THE THRESHOLD

Any young man could have written the letters that Melvin wrote home during the early years of the war. His words no doubt echoed many of the same stories read in homes all across America back then. At times, it is like reading a daily diary.

But because the words were penned in my father's hand, they held such a special meaning for me. The opportunity to learn more about life back then was one thing, but to read his words telling the story was a gift.

I enjoy showing my favorite picture of him to anyone who will take an interest in the past. I have to admit, sometimes showing his picture is when the past becomes interesting.

Melvin was one of those men who was always dressed to the nines as they used to say. On any given day, he was wearing a suit and tie. His hair was trained with tonic and combed exactly to his liking and his confidence in how he looked was evident. He knew he looked good. And so did all of the young women who knew him and were vying for his attention.

His demeanor appeared to be a little on the cocky side and more often than not, his parents had given in to his every whim. I don't think he ever had to answer to anyone. Until January of 1943 when his military 'career' began that is.

Melvin had been out of school for almost four years before joining the Army Air Corps. During that time, he never really found himself; however, I don't think he was looking all that hard.

My favorite picture of my father

Melvin, January 1943

His first letter home is from Nashville, Tennessee. Keep in mind that I have deleted any irrelevant portions. From the time that both men entered the service until they leave for overseas, I have let Melvin's letters take over for the most part, adding Clarence's stories based on the timeline.

January 19, 1943 Nashville TN

Dear Dad,

S'pose you're plenty lonely now. But it's all for the best, Dad - I can see right now we're here to go to it, and I'm standing on the threshold of something. There isn't much to tell. We were 21 hours on the train. We're only three miles from Nashville.

We'll be in quarantine for two weeks. We can't receive mail, so don't write. I like it here, but would rather be in Texas.

I chose pilot for first choice, navigator and then bombardier.

We're confined in quarantine in one spot till 2 weeks are up. Can't leave the area 'til then unless we go in a big detail.

It doesn't seem like I'm 850 miles apart from you.

I look good in my uniform. Officer hat and large wings on it. And blue band around it. There are planes flying all over all day. I guess I'm in the Air Force alright.

Your best son, Mel

Melvin as a young cadet

Clarence didn't have much to say until it came to Tennessee Maneuvers early in 1944 but there were a few exceptions. He said again that he wished he had kept a diary of the war years. It is because Melvin wrote so many letters home that it is like a diary and so much more information than Clarence could remember.

January 24, 1943 Nashville TN

Dear Dad -

We've been in quarantine since Tuesday. We have two weeks altogether. We wear handkerchiefs over our mouths and noses to prevent measles. If anyone in our squadron (210 men) gets them we're still in quarantine for two weeks after the day the fellow gets them. Everyone's keeping their fingers crossed, and I don't mean maybe.

These barracks inspections are a bitch. You can't have any dust on your shoes. The officer comes through. You pop to, and stay there, or else. He runs his finger across your shoes and the shelves. They better be clean or you get a gig. Four of them and you walk it off, resolving not to let it happen again.

Your uniforms have to be hung on clothes hangers with all the buttons buttoned, pockets and all, or else.

I took my test yesterday I mentioned before. Eight in the A.M. 'til 4:45 in the P.M. and an hour off for lunch. Seven hours and 45 minutes. I was really punchy when I got done. I thought I had a little education, but now I think it was damn little. I felt like a high class moron when I got done.

Tomorrow morning I take more tests on co-ordination and quick thinking. Also a doctor questions us, and then in a few days we start physicals. Most of them wash out in the Schneider index.

Love, your best son, Mel

January 31, 1943 Nashville TN

Dear Dad

I just got off of guard duty at 4:00 P.M. Plenty tired. 2 hours on and 4 off. The damn gas mask weighs a ton by the time you're through. Tomorrow I go up for my classification.

We're getting precision drilling. No rifle teams yet, though. Won't write much as I'm badly in need of sleep. Guard takes it out of you.

Nervous as a cat. Hope I make navigator. They get 2nd lieutenant. Higher than flight officer. Navigator also gets flying time so he can land planes in case of emergency. He's really a valuable man.

Love, Mel

February 1, 1943 Nashville TN

I've finally passed. I was recommended for a navigator. We get 27 weeks training, and then graduate a 2nd Lt.

That's superior rank to flight officer. Some fun. We can pick up flying time on cross country runs when we get advanced enough. We also go to gunnery school, and a few other details.

Love from your son, Mel

PRE-FLIGHT – SHOOTING
DOTS AND DASHES

Melvin's next stop is Selman Field in Monroe Louisiana. Construction of this AAF base began in June of 1942 and was a rapidly built priority due to wartime conditions. In no time at all, the airstrips, hangars, barracks, clinics and hospitals to name a few necessities were built and servicemen began arriving by train. Only at Selman could a cadet receive his entire training from pre-flight to advanced.

All branches of the service, then and now, train with a purpose. My husband and both sons are former Marines. I once watched a video of the first five minutes of a new recruit's life after arriving in San Diego at the Marine Corps Recruiting Depot. There aren't words to describe five minutes let alone all of basic training.

Later, I commented to my husband that it must have been difficult to watch our sons join knowing what it would be like for them. He said, "But they didn't know. None of us did. It wasn't so you could go out and drill and look pretty. It was so you could learn to take orders. They were training you for those few minutes, few hours or few days when you may need it."

February 6, 1943 Selman Field, Monroe LA

Dear Dad,

This is pre-flight. I'll be here 9 weeks. I'm now starting on my 27 weeks. Nashville didn't count.

Then I'll either be sent across the street to the advanced class or I'll go to Coral Gables Florida or to gunnery school. Navigators have to take gunnery too as well as radio, wildcat flying, ballistics, attack maneuvers, cross country, etc.

We received instruction in the .30 caliber Johnson machine gun, .45 colt pistol and British Enfield rifle.

Selman Field is a mile from here. Sky is black with planes.

On our cross-country practice flying, we'll hop all over Texas, Georgia, Alabama, Mississippi, Arkansas, Kentucky, and Tennessee.

On nearing our graduation, we'll fly one long one. New York City or somewhere.

Write, Love Mel

February 19, 1943 Selman Field, Monroe LA

Dear Dad,

Well, school tomorrow till 11 - Then parade from 1 to 2 in full dress. Then a typhoid shot at the hospital at 2. Then I'm free to go into Monroe till 2:30 AM Sunday morn. Monroe is in the northern part of LA. We're 3 miles east of it. Buses run out here.

I received a letter from you that was held up at Nashville. I suggest you number them. I'll do the same. Then we'll know if one is missing. Ok?

They got a joint in town called the Cascades. I've heard a lot about it, and am anxious to see it.

They gave us the "Burma Road" today. The damn thing is appropriately named too. Five miles long, and all hills and rough terrain up and down, in and out.

Our schedule is getting stiffer. Last nite we learned how to take the .45 pistol apart and together in record time. I practiced the operation again and again till I became expert at it.

Then we got the Thompson sub-machine gun. We have to be able to rip them down too. Some sh-t. She weighs 10 ¾ #. I carried one around last nite, and they get plenty heavy. I 'spose we'll get rifle drill p.d.q. now.

We'll get classes to replace the ones we drop next week. 'Spose one will be meteorology or first aid. We just received a Weem's plotter for navigation today. Know what it's for? Neither do I_____yet.

Love, Your son, Mel

February 22, 1943 Selman Field, Monroe LA

Today we had a short day - Only fourteen hours. Got over at 8:20 tonite with classes. We got a lecture on the dangers and aids of stratosphere flying.

I guess we'll get pressure chamber next week. That'll be hot stuff.

We're getting first aid now. We've all got to be qualified as there's no doc's on the bombers.

(In this section of his letter, he asked his Dad if he knew any code and proceeded to write a half a page of Morse code.)

Figure that out for the hell of it. Love, Mel

March 1, 1943 Selman Field, Monroe LA

Three cadets and a flight officer (navigator), and a 2nd Lt (pilot) left here this morning on a training run. They crashed near Hondo Texas and all were killed instantly. Too bad, but it happens to the best of them. Nothing will happen to me though as I'm too darn ornery.

In math we're studying drift angles, drift corrections, courses, heading, air speed, ground speech, wind velocity, and triangular velocities. It's easy once you catch on. We've also got physics and meteorology. Any day we get the pressure chamber. Last week a guy passed out, and they had to drop the whole chamber to get him, as the emergency lock was also being used.

All the guys were jumping up and down screaming. A lot of them passed out.

Still have got code and aircraft identification. They flash a picture on the screen for 1/25 of a second. You have to know it. Later on they'll step it up to 1/100 of a second. Sounds impossible, but it isn't. Some of the guys have trouble, but I knew 90% of them before I came in. They give us six digit numbers as 976583, and we get them at 1/25. They claim you can get 13 digits like 7654286326548 at 1/100 with training. I think so. You're eyes become a camera, and afterwards, you think of what you've seen. I find it so already. They flashed a German Focke-Wulfe 190 on the screen the other day with British markings on it. I was the only one who knew what it was.

A fellow in my suite went to the hospital with measles this morning. I 'spose we'll be quarantined again. Hot dog.

Send me that article will ya? We had to fill out publication forms when we got here. I think they sent them in. I was against it, but, he had bars on, and poor little me didn't.

Love to you Dad, Mel

Postcard from Selman Field showing class for aircraft identification

On the back of the postcard is printed: Know your aircraft. Shooting up friendly planes, or allowing enemy planes to go unrecognized, will not help win the war. To avoid these errors, there's only one thing to do – learn to recognize airplanes of all types and nationalities. Classes such as this, with the aid of slides, silhouettes, pictures and models, give the cadet this essential knowledge.

March 7, 1943 Selman Field, Monroe LA

Well, came through the pressure chamber ok. Eighteen started, and five passed out. We were up at 38,000 feet, and one passed out in the first 15 minutes. I was a guinea pig. Went without oxygen starting at 18,000 feet. Had to write my serial no and name at every thousand foot rise. Got to 28,000 feet and lasted 3 ½ min. before I couldn't even write a damn thing. Everything was turning black, and I started to weave. Then the instructor turned on my oxygen. I had an instrument on my ear attached to a photo-electric cell chart. It showed the oxygen content in my blood as it descended. It went from a normal 96 to an 80. Seventy-five is the real danger point.

Had the stiffest cross-country run of all today. Right after breakfast. We all got sick. Thirteen of us finished out of 37. Two more blocks, and I wouldn't have lasted.

A.S.N. means Army Serial Number.

I'm in Squadron "H" now. Everyone is changed around. I've still have my same roommate, though. All six in my suite came along.

We've dropped meteorology until we get into advanced school. From now on, we don't have school on Sat. They'll cook up something else, no doubt.

By the way, they're also going to make bombardiers out of us.

We'll be real men when we get through. That means an additional 12 weeks training.

Well, Dad. All for now and will write more later.

Love, Mel

March 18, 1943 Selman Field, Monroe LA

Dear Dad,

Went through actual attacks of mustard, chloropicrin, phosgene and lewisite gases yesterday. Not bad. Eyes smarted a little.

Taking chemical warfare as a sideline.

Today our ear code ends, tonite visual blinker starts. Means nite classes. No fun. All outdoors. Do I write jerky? All is jerky and fast down here. You get that way I guess.

Well, I'll see ya'.

Be good, Love Mel

March 24, 1943 Selman Field, Monroe LA

Dear Dad,

I'm supposed to be in visual code class right now. It's held outside at night. They shoot dots and dashes with a light gun at a half a mile. We've finished all our code by ear. Last week. Have a final exam on math tomorrow. Everything we've had so far. Then we start the E-6-B computer. It figures winds, air speeds, ground speeds, radius of action, rate of closure, rate of departure, and a couple dozen other things. Don't 'spose you know what those are, but it's all navigation.

We've got the communications procedure to learn now. I've got it all memorized. They have definite words to mean definite things. I'll write more next week Dad. We've had a very rigorous week. One test after another.

Saturday I have my last tetanus. Then I'm all done. Typhoid was done 2 weeks ago. Have to take a makeup final in maps and charts.

Tomorrow we have tests on photography. No fun. I hate cameras.

Hope I can go to gunnery before I go to advanced. It's only 5 weeks, but I guess they're packed with math on trajectories, leads, firepower's, relative speeds of attacking aircraft in relation to yours etc. A lot of fun though.

FORT JACKSON

UNIT HISTORY REPORT: The 106th Division was activated on March 15, 1943, at Fort Jackson, South Carolina. According to this report, a study was made in September of that same year, and it revealed the fact that two-thirds of the entire enlisted personnel was 22 years of age or under; more than three-quarters of the men were 25 years of age or under.

Basic training was at Fort Jackson from March 29th to July 10th. Emphasis was on physical conditioning, small unit tactical training and marksmanship. Individual training included digging foxholes and slit trenches, identification of aircraft and tanks, map and compass reading and many lectures given by renowned figures. The report does not state who those figures were. However, the Division was complimented on the manner in which its members had executed the tests.

Clarence remembers the maneuvers held at Fort Jackson as being just a prelude to the famous Tennessee maneuvers that the 106th went through about a year later. This following picture is of, you guessed it. All of the men lined up, as he said to me, "for the crapper."

I don't think he is in this one. Or maybe he is 'in' where you can't see him? He wasn't sure either if one of the men pictured was him or not.

The make-shift 'restroom' on maneuvers in Fort Jackson

This next picture is also taken at Fort Jackson of Clarence. He never said if this was his barracks or not. I visited Fort Jackson a while back and took a few pictures. Some of the buildings looked the same according to Clarence, but there were also a lot of changes.

Clarence at Fort Jackson

There seemed to be plaques everywhere for divisions that trained at Fort Jackson so of course I was determined to find the one for the 106th. I was just about to think I would have to drive around for a while to find it when a wrong turn took me right to it.

While there, I obtained a map from 1942 which I brought home for Clarence. He said some of it seemed familiar, some did not. That was to be expected. He reminded me again that it had been a long time since he was there.

Once they were able to obtain a pass and go into Columbia, one of the things Clarence did was get his shoes shined as in the following picture. On one copy he wrote, 'me and my shoeshine boys.'

Clarence in Columbia, South Carolina, having his shoes shined

I QUIT

Dad,

Today is Sunday. 'Spose you're sitting day dreaming, or perhaps worrying. Day dreaming is all right, worrying isn't.

Don't worry about me Dad. I'm swell and I've just graduated from pre-flight. I'm now in the advanced school. Every Sat. we'll have 3 hours of exams and every third Sat. a 7 hour exam. Some fun. No more fooling around. This is it. The real McCoy. Nine weeks in, and eighteen to go. Four and one half short, hard months.

We turned in everything yesterday morning, and were reissued a lot of it over here plus a lot more brand new. Our computers were also brand new and made in Canada consigned to the RCAF. We got them instead.

We also got wrist watches. Navigation 'hack' watches (worth $75.00.) A stop second hand for resetting to correct time. The most they ever lose is 5 seconds a day. We keep a chart on their accuracy. In the air you deal in seconds.

A lot of the guys are wondering if they'll get airsick. They've never been up, a lot of them. I wouldn't have joined without going up first.

New address - A/c Melvin Pollock
          A.A.F.N.S. Class 43-11
          Flight 66, Squadron 6
          Selman Field, Monroe La

I'm 1/3 of a navigator now. Happy day!

Love to you Dad, Mel

April 19, 1943 Selman Field, Monroe LA

Dad,

I'm back in the old groove again. Business has slacked off. I got demerits for not being shaved at retreat. Hardly anyone got away scott-free. I shaved last nite, but they grow to beat hell.

Send me that old box camera of ours. You can't buy one for love or money down here. At least not for money. (I haven't tried the other yet!)

Wish you could be here for my graduation. We'll see. I think it can be arranged.

You must really be proud of that diploma to frame it. I really earned that damn thing all in all though, at that.

From your best son, Mel

May 4, 1943 Selman Field, Monroe LA

Dad,

Well, we flew Monday. Not so bad. We went over into Mississippi to Oxford. Then into Little Rock, Arkansas cutting across Tennessee.

I used three types of navigation. Dead reckoning, follow the pilot, and pilotage.

Coming back, our radio went dead, and the drift meters went out. Then we flew by using check points. Came in ok too. We were up 4 ½ hours. Covered plenty of territory too.

Tomorrow we go up again. We'll fly 200 feet off the ground at consecutive speeds using a stop watch to calibrate our air speed meter.

Some of the guys were sicker 'n a dog. One guy with me was plenty sick. He'd never been up before.

Then we've got the upper class system now since Monday. They'll come up and say "What're you famous for mister? You'll say "Sawing toilet seats in half for half assed upper classmen, or eating ex-lax and feathers so I can tickle the shit out of myself."

Love, Mel

May 12, 1943 Selman Field, Monroe LA

Dear Pa,

Flew our third mission yesterday. Ok. Got a front tooth knocked out on the landing. Just cracked off 2/3 of the way up. It'll be easy to fix. They'll put a ¾ enamel crown on. It looks like hell personified. I was in the co-pilot's seat, and was finishing my log. We hit hard, and my jaws snapped together.

We were over Dallas Texas yesterday. Averaged 180 m.p.h. over, and 197 back. Tail wind back.

We've got interception, searches, and radius of action to alternate aircraft carriers now. No fun!

Got the camera out of the post office today. First chance I had. It's been there three days.

I could write you a book on what I've learned, but it isn't interesting unless you know the terms.

You ought to see these barracks. I wouldn't keep horses in them. But here I am living in them. You roast by day, and wake up in the morning, and have to chip the icicles off before you can get out of bed.

I listened to dance bands all during the flights yesterday. Got them on the compass radio. They're good outfits. About $10,000 a piece per plane.

Love from your son, Mel

May 31, 1943 Selman Field, Monroe LA

Dad,

I've decided to quit navigation. I've done alright by it, but I can't get interested in it anymore. I can't see myself sitting up there at a desk, when I could have guns or anything else to occupy my time. I just wasn't cut out for this damn work.

I don't really like to be a quitter, Dad, but after all, if I had a job in civilian life I didn't like, I'd get another. This is the very same thing to me.

I'd like aerial gunnery, as the action appeals to me. But it goes down on my record that I asked out of navigation. I'll be automatically out of air crew. So I asked my instructor if he could fix that. He said he could make it into a washout. I said that'd be ok with me.

I'm sure not sorry to be out of it. I'm glad. I considered it from all angles before I decided. I've got it in my grasp, but what do I do? I sweep it away with one motion.

Funny thing, I don't give a damn for those bars any more. All I want is for this war to end so I can go into art.

I don't know what in hell I want, and that's the truth. Maybe this army is changing me.

Sometimes I wonder what in hell is the matter with me. I can't dig into things like I should.

Did I ever see a wreck May 27th. A B-26 "Marauder" was taking off on the southern runway. It got about 50' off the ground and done in. It exploded and burned and killed seven people. We all stood there like wooden Indians. Five died instantly, and the other two lived but a few minutes.

Love to you Dad, Mel

My grandfather was 'a bit disappointed' as he put it when he received this letter about Melvin quitting navigation. He had been boasting about his accomplishments and all that he was learning to everyone he talked to at the barber shop he worked at.

Melvin knew he felt bad, but he stood by his decision. Until later.

HIGH SCHOOL GRADUATION

My mother was beautiful as far as I'm concerned. No wonder both of these men fell in love with her.

Lucille graduated from high school on June 3, 1943. Because she was no longer afraid to be away from home, she immediately went to work in Chicago and held a few different jobs while there. Grace and some of their cousins had already set up housekeeping and were having the time of their lives.

Their cousin, Flo, kept a diary and every entry was more enjoyable to read than the last. It was December of 1943 that she wrote about Clarence being home on furlough and he had given Lucille a bracelet for Christmas. Lucille doesn't remember this, but it must be so because Flo had written it down. Grace remembered it, also.

Clarence would have done anything at the time to make sure she never forgot him. He was in love, but she was too busy having fun and apparently not really paying much attention to anyone in particular. She was so young and now that she was brave enough to have ventured out into the world, she was going to make the most of it. How fun for all of them. I have always said that there is nothing like cousins to spend some very valuable time with.

Clarence home on leave at Christmas time

Besides working a variety of jobs not only in Chicago but all over, when she came back home for a time, she, Grace and my grandmother worked at Badger Ordnance. The three of them would drive to White Creek, a small town along Hwy 13, and catch a bus that took all of the workers to the plant. After a while, they rented an apartment in Sauk in order to make it easier because of the hours.

Lucille said they worked swing shifts, six weeks at a time and six days a week. The hours were from 8-4, 4-12 and 12-8 and they made eighty-seven cents an hour. They were doing their part for the war effort along with everyone else but of course now the pay sure doesn't seem like it was much.

Lucille's graduation picture, June 1943

ALCATRAZ

I came to the conclusion early on that there wasn't too much I could actually contribute when it came to what I consider the training years. Oh, I have added something here and there, but it seemed to me that for the most part, I should just let Melvin's letters take over.

My other thought was, since he was a great writer who hoped to publish his work one day, why not do this together. Keep in mind that he wasn't worried about editing. He was writing home.

June 21, 1943 Keesler Field, Biloxi MS

Dad,

Balls, but I really did myself up proud this time. I've been here since Sat. & this is Monday, and I hate it like nobody's business!

Walter Winchell once called this dump "the Alcatraz of the Army". I sure as hell know what he meant. It's all around me.

I took a test today for O.C.S. and college training. You have to score 110 for O.C.S. (Officers Candidate School), and 115 for the college program. It's only a forty minute test for 150 questions. I scored 135. I got the highest mark of the 13 who took it. You never had any dumb kids.

I don't know if you're blue, but I know I am. Maybe we can cheer each other up in our solitude, Dad. How about it?

The Gulf's really pretty, hey? I saw it coming in. We got in Gulfport Sat. aft. at 12:30. Then caught a bus for the last 12 miles to Keesler Field. Our luggage just came today.

Tomorrow we get issued helmets, canteens, jackets, etc. Some fun. Leggings, mess kits.

One thing about the army, you sure develop an outlook on life. And how!

Love Mel

June 24, 1943 Keesler Field MS

Dad,

Yesterday we went out on an overnite march. Eight goddamn miles out to the rifle range and back today. My feet are pretty sore. Not used to it. I'm pretty damn tired.

This morning we fired the new M-1 officer's and noncoms carbine. A honey. It can be brought into action faster than a man can draw a pistol. No recoil or anything.

Then we fired the Thompson sub-machine gun. I've always wanted to fire a machine gun, and now I have.

I had a clip of 30, and I just squeezed the trigger, and they were gone before I released it. Some fun.

Each of us carried half of a pup tent, 5 stakes, a rope, blanket, canteen, mess kit, etc.

You can get up any damn time you want to as long as it's not later than 5:15 A.M. The food is pretty lousy. In fact everything is.

Out in the bush for two days. I'm here listening to a radio catching up with the outside world. Boy, I mean bush, too. If you've ever been in Mississippi, you'll know what I mean.

If anyone ever catches me south of the Mason-Dixon line when this fracas is all over, they can just put me in the bug house for sure without even giving me the entrance exam.

It's a damn good thing I've still got a sense of humor. Or have I? I ask myself. No answer.

Geez, I'm getting' nuttier than a dime store fruit cake from this army.

You ought to see me, I'm as brown as an Indian and in pretty fair shape.

Love from your best son, Mel

June 28, 1943 Keesler Field MS

Dear Dad,

Well, I'm scheduled to ship Wednesday morning at 11:30. Our destination is #3603. Wherever in hell that is. I don't know. 'Spose I'll have to send that foot locker to you tomorrow. We might even go across the street. Christ would I ever hate that. There's a possibility we'll get mechanics. They'll never make a mechanic out of me. I'll see to that.

They said I'd make a good armament man as I'd worked with all micrometers at the lathe.

I've been building machine gun nests out at the airport. Work about 10 minutes a day. Kind of a boss I guess.

I watched them test 3 Tomahawk P-40's the other day. They'd come 300 miles an hour 10 feet off the ground across the airport about 50 to 100 feet from us. Some fun!! For the first time I really enjoyed myself.

The air corps is a helluva place to be if you're on the ground.

Love Mel

20/20

July 13, 1943 Amarillo Army Air Field, Amarillo TX

Well, here I am in Texas. I guess we came over 1,000 miles. We're over 1,130 miles from Chicago. Forty-two hours of travel.

We went to Gulfport, Mississippi. Then along the coast to New Orleans. Our train was blacked out. Army regulations. No subs can use the lights for guides. I was plenty tired as we didn't have Pullmans.

We'll be in mechanic's school. We'll be crew chiefs. Flying sergeants. We'll all be aerial gunners too. I took the "63" physical. Your eyes have to be perfect. Guess what. My eyes are all ok again. 20-20. Ain't that wonderful? I think so. I don't believe I ever did have astigmatism. I never did get those glasses.

We were in New Orleans a while. Walked uptown, and it's ok. From New Orleans to Alexandria, Shreveport, and into Marshall, Texas. Then to Longview. West of there I saw miles and miles of oil derricks.

I like this place better than any of the others.

We can't even get beer in town until they get some more shipped in. I'll have to write my congressman about it.

'Spose I should thank this ole army for all the travel, but somehow I can't.

Well, I'm a P.F.C. now. That's 4.00 a month more. It all helps.

We have six weeks of gunnery coming up after AM school. They make crew chiefs out of these guys. We'll be S/Sgts with flying pay.

No chance for a furlough now. Just ready to start school anyway.

Love, Mel

What I do know is that Melvin had his dad getting recommendation letters from home from anyone they thought might be influential. He had changed his mind about the cadets and wanted to try again. Well actually, it was because he now knew his eyes were fine.

August 29, 1943 Amarillo TX

Dear Dad,

Haven't really much to say. Still haven't heard from the cadet board. Won't for over a week yet.

Heard they lowered the requirements for the cadets considerably. Spose they have, now that

I've taken the pains to pass it 20-20. That's life for ya'.

Should make it back in the cadets. Sure hope I do.

If I get in, I'm going to ask for a furlough. Maybe I'll get it, too. I've been in over 7 months and haven't even had a three day pass yet. That rates something.

Love, Mel

September 4, 1943 Amarillo TX

Dear Dad,

When I got back from the hospital today everyone had a form that had to be filled out for the cadets. They've got a big drive on to get more. Guess they really want them. They must be building a lot of planes to be so short on men. All that is really very encouraging. Think I'll make it.

Love to you Dad, Mel

September 10, 1943 Amarillo TX

Dear Paw,

About this cadet business. I don't give myself much chance of getting back in. They've been turning down too many ex-cadets.

I'm going up in the morning to see if my letter came back. It really should have by now.

They've really got the school all screwed up now. There're 44 of us in our class, and 2 have to stay out of school every day for details. Then they wash back. Every 22 days we're all together again.

I'm really getting tired of this nite shift.

Be good Dad,

Mel xxxooo

September 13, 1943 Amarillo TX

Well, I got my letter back from the cadets, and it's out. They're refusing all ex-cadets. Or at least 94% of them. Makes me kind of disgusted.

Guess I'll have to go thru this damn school to get out. Either that or die. Only two ways.

I've hit on the notion I'd like to go to Paris after this war. There's another guy here who wants to go. He's going to study art after the war. He's pretty good at it. Different style than mine tho.

Not much to write. Tomorrow is our day off. I'll maybe go to Pampa. It's smaller, but not many soldiers go over there. It's an advanced flying school. The cadets only get out on Sunday, so we'll have our own little way.

Don't know how I'll get a damn commission out of this war, as I guess I'll have to go overseas a gunner, and knock hell out of some Jap zeros, get decorated, and ask for the cadets again. Joke.

Love to you, Dad. Mel

September 23, 1943 Amarillo TX

Dad,

Well, I'm over half-way thru this dump. Sixty days gone of school and 52 to go. This is one of the longest tech schools to go thru. I guess I've learned a lot, and all that, but I really don't appreciate it. All I've done is go to schools. 'Spose I'll be a smart punk and all that, as I've had a lot of school after high school. 13 weeks N.Y.A. 18 of nav., and 10 of this. That's 41 weeks. Plus being an usher in a theatre, several gas stations, Nye Picus, Briggs & Stratton, and Hercules Powder Co.

Heard we either go to factory school, or gunnery. That's 12 weeks now instead of six. Factory school is a month. They say it's really nice. Don't snake your beds at all. Just sit all day and listen, and help assemble planes and learn.

Love, Mel

September 23, 1943 Amarillo TX

Dad,

I go on a detail tomorrow. Tear up a smashed B-17F. Will wash back a class and all that, but we'll all get it so will still graduate together.

My partner volunteered so he could stay with me. Nice of him.

Love to you Dad, Mel

October 10, 1943 Amarillo TX

Dear Dad,

They called me out of school yesterday. Outside was waiting a kid from my old flight at Selman. 2nd Lt. He told me old Howie Raaven was killed 2 weeks ago at Dalhart. Raaven was a real good friend of mine, and I was damned sorry to hear it. Plane dragged a wing, and exploded & burned. It was all foggy for two days, and there were five crashes killing 17 of 18 crewmen. Bad.

He sure made me wish I'd kept at it. Wings, bars, & $291.00 a month. Especially the dough.

Only 39 days left now. Happy day!

Can't get over Raaven. Hard.

Love, Mel xxxxx

October 16, 1943 Amarillo TX

Dear Dad -

Well, only 35 days of this nuthouse left. Then I'll be free for a little while.

Then it's gunnery, or factory school, & then gunnery. I'd like to skip that damn factory school. I'm getting sick of schools.

I've had 30 weeks of school so far in this man's army. I'll be a little smarter maybe, but the fact still remains that there is some things that you wouldn't give a damn to learn, & mech & nav are two of them as far as I'm concerned.

We've been testing engines for 9 days now. All day I test engines, and all nite my ears ring like church bells. Good thing I'm the only one who can hear them, or they'd keep the whole barracks awake.

Sitting here on the floor writing on my locker. What a pose - What a picture!

Love, Mel xxxxx

October 18, 1943 Amarillo TX

Dad,

Only 32 days left. Just finished 80 of 'em.

Was looking at the guys just starting in tonite. Wouldn't swap for the world.

Guess I won't be home for another 3 or 4 months. Have to go to gunnery first.

The guys who are finishing AM & have been to gunnery are getting 10 day furloughs. Lucky guys.

We're on engine change now. Have 6 more days of that left. At least my ears don't ring now at nite.

Saw a B-26 Marauder painted bright yellow today. Looked funny. Imagine it's a navy plane. First one I've seen that color.

Love, Mel xxxooo

October 21, 1943 Amarillo TX

Paw,

Well, it's official now. All men qualified for gunnery will go, and no factory school. Gunnery is six weeks, and then we'll have a furlough for 10 days, and maybe even 4 days traveling time. All the guys who have been to gunnery will have furlough upon completion here.

I've washed back another class. They decided the one I was in was too big, and washed 42 of us back to the next one. It doesn't really make any great difference.

Be good, Dad.

Love, Mel

October 25, 1943 Amarillo TX

Dad,

Pretty soon I'll be out of this place. That'll be a red letter day for the Irish.

Another day off today and nothing to do. Nothing in town even if I wasn't broke. Payday is only 8 days off and then I'll celebrate.

We'll be out by Thanksgiving unless things slide back again.

Love to you Dad,

Mel

November 11, 1943 Amarillo TX

Dear Dad -

That last ten days we spend out in the field diving into fox holes at pretended bombing attacks. Hell, ten days to learn how to dive into a foxhole. They must think we're pretty ignorant.

Saw a new B-29 bomber last week. All of the gun turrets are operated by remote control. There's six superchargers. One for each of 4 motors, and 2 for the cabin. It's all sealed & will fly in the stratosphere. They said they'll send 7 of our 34 men to B-29 school. Might be commissions in it as flight engineer. I'm going to refuse it if it's offered me. Don't care to even go near it...Three months of electrical, and three of B-29, and then remote control gunnery. Don't want it. I'm sick of school.

The B-17F is a heavy bomber. We'll probably be gunners on it, as we went to B-17 school.

The B-17 has a wing span of 103 feet 9 inches and a length of 78 feet 8 inches. Big, huh?

Take care, Dad.

Love, Mel

November 23, 1943 Amarillo TX

Dear Dad,

We have 2 days of school left. Galvin graduated yesterday. Said it left him time to go into town but no money. Lost 45.00 in a poker game. You'd think he'd send his ma some of that if he just blows it like that.

Don't know if we'll ship out immediately or not. Have heard yes & no, so what to believe? These goddamn rumor mongers here don't know a damn thing about it. See all, tell all, & know nothing.

Was in a B-26 bomber today. Took the guns off the walls and mounted them. Just monkeying around. Nice plane. It won't fly on paper. Figures are against it. It's pretty hot on landings.

That one that crashed at Monroe and killed 7 was a B-26.

Field test is the bunk. Just wind & dust.

You don't learn a damn thing.

Saw Joe Louis give an exhibition in a hangar tonite with Geo. Nicholson. Also Jackie Wilson & another guy. Ray Robinson was also 'sposed to appear but didn't. Louis looks a little fat, but not soft.

We'll either go to Tyndall, Florida, Kingman, Arizona, Harlingen, Texas, or Las Vegas, Nevada for gunnery. Hope it's Fla. as it's plenty chilly even this far north. Should be gone in a week. Hope so, anyway—

Love Mel

This next picture is taken in Amarillo and Melvin writes on the back; 'Peak of our military careers. Hah-hah!' It was taken on November 26, 1943.

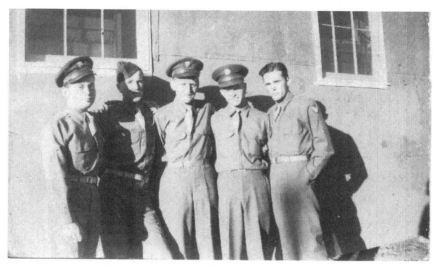

McTavey, Patterson, Matlock, Palmer and Melvin

November 27, 1943

Dear Dad,

Well, we're leaving soon for gunnery. I guess it's Las Vegas, Nev. In fact, I'm sure it is.

Just heard on the radio about a gal in Claremont, Minnesota that ran around the table, and every time she went around she slashed at her 3 year old kid with a butcher knife, killing the kid finally. What a gal! You can talk about your freaks in the world, but the human mind is the queerest of them all, if you should happen to ask me.

66

For once I won't be adding any new states to my list when I move. Oh, well, I've been in half of them anyway.

Love, Mel xxxooo

I'M SKEPTICAL

Sat - December 4, 1943 Las Vegas NV

Dad,

Well, here I am at a new post. My fifth. We'll start school probably in a week. Sooner or later.

I was right on my hunch on where'd we go. There was no change in orders.

We went on the Santa Fe to Clovis, N.M. and on over to Gallup. Then on to Williams, Ariz and Seligman, Flagstaff, & Kingman. Then to Barstow Calif. where we switched on up to Las Vegas. The same route we've been over before, isn't it?

The trip took 50 hours. We had Pullmans & it wasn't half bad. No use in telling you what it looks like down here, as you've seen it all. There's mountains all around us, & it sure is a welcome change from that barren table we were on for 5 months.

The school is 7 weeks. Then we are issued flying clothes and bags, & are sent to a replacement center at Salt Lake. I should get a nice furlough then.

I should have gotten a shoe stamp while at Amarillo. You can't get them here, as only officers are entitled to lo-cuts. Hells bells!

Also you have to turn in an old tube to get tooth paste, etc. First time I've run into that too.

I have to get some sun glasses sooner or later, as soon as I can get ahold of some dough. The sun is pretty bright here, alongside of that white sand that reflects it to beat hell.

There isn't a helluva lot to scrawl about as I don't know too much about the field yet.

Sure are a lot of planes here. Lot of different types too. Some for turret firing & others for standing & firing.

I sure will be ready to throw this uniform off as soon as I can when this war is all over. I'm sick of the damn army & I don't give a damn who knows it, either... Guess you can tell that anyway by my letters, can't you?

I lost a kid that has been with me thru Monroe, La. Pre-flite and all. We were together nine months. Hugh Palmer from Sanford, N.C.

He got to monkeying around with the cadet board trying to see if he could get back in. It kept him off the shipping list. He was in my same class in Monroe. Quit just 3 days after I did.

We'll only be corporal when we get thru here. Only cpl. since Nov. 1. Used to be 3 stripes. Now only 2. Stripes are getting harder to earn all the time. But, what's the difference? The answer is $12.00 pay.

Love to you, Dad.

Mel

Melvin's talent for words is very evident in this next letter. I am so certain that had he lived, he would have finished the two books he started and even would have written more. I know he would have continued to draw. His sketches are pretty amazing.

I am so impressed by his words and I am certain you will be, too. They are rather mind-boggling for lack of a better description and of course there is humor in the letter as usual.

December 8, 1943 Las Vegas NV

Dear Dad,

Guess I have been slightly lax in my letter writing of late. For one thing, we were on that field test 11 days & I never exactly felt like writing after 12 hrs. out there in the wind. You understand, don't you?

Still waiting to go to school & don't know when we'll start. It'll probably be on a Monday. I mean next

Monday. There's a class every Mon. starts. You need 545 men for a squadron.

Well, I see I've been rated for the good conduct medal. All of which is hard to earn. Only 1,365,000 men have one. It means that I've eaten my Wheaties 1 year in a row every morning. All you have to do is stay sober, & keep away from an M.P.

I've also got a sharpshooter's medal coming to me for the carbine. I was 8 under expert. You need 175 out of 200. I had 167. I've never worn it, but it will be on my blouse when I get home. The girls go for it. Little do they know, the dears.

A military expert is a G.I. who concentrates more & more on less and less until he knows practically everything about nothing.

We go over every nite, & load up on beer at the P.X. (Post Exchange.) Then we proceed home gaily & pour ourselves into bed.

How about this crazy life? I'm skeptical.

Everything about us is false, & conventional - all a matter of lies which we are forced to accept. People love music and poetry as though they were divine & eternal. If the structure of our ears were altered in the slightest, the symphonies of Beethoven would become a regular din; if our retinas were to change in their functioning, we would just as aloof burn the greatest masterpieces of the age as not, as they would appear as so many canvasses dirtied by a child's hands; if our brains were modified, the greatest thinkers & writers of the world would appear as idiots who were bathing themselves with a glory that covered nonsensical things.

Illusions are a lie, but I want them near me; hope is another, but I want it to walk before me always.

Wonder when we'll get into Las Vegas. Hope soon. This sitting around like a stick in the mud when there's lites only 10 miles hence, sure as hell never was for me.

Everyone thinks the Air Corps is glamorous, but we know different, hey? I'll take a job and money, etc.

Take care of yourself old boy, & I'll write again soon.

Love, Your son, Mel xxxxx

Wed - 12-15-'43 Las Vegas NV

Dear dad-

Well, I was just up in front of the Lt. for sleeping late, along with about 39 others. We have 2 hours of drill at 1:00 P.M. Sunday.

I had my last wisdom tooth pulled yest. afternoon. Not much to it. Just froze it & yanked it. The hole is closed already.

We're making our runs at the pressure chamber again at 3:00 this aft. We were up yest. morning for an hour, & the guy next to me turned pale, & cold sweat broke out on his face. He tried to tell me afterward he was ok. I know better. He had anoxia.

We were at 20,000 at the time, & without oxygen for twelve minutes at a time. Anoxia is oxygen lack. Your vision fades & you keel over. Without O2 at 38,000 you'd be unconscious in 30 seconds, & dead in 2 or 3 minutes. At 20,000 you can last 30 minutes before keeling over, and another ½ hour alive. Maybe a little more.

We were up to 30,000'. You only get bends over that. Today we go up to the bends altitude. Bends is what divers get by coming to the surface too fast. Nitrogen bubbles press on your nerves & create pain by decrease in pressure. Increased pressure compresses the N2 bubbles & bends disappear.

I was all thru the chamber in Monroe, La in pre-flite. That stuff never bothers me, but I've seen 'em lugged into the emergency lock colder than a mackerel.

The last war lasted 1, 766 days. This is the 1,767th day of this one. That's since 1939, of course, before we were in it.

How long were you in the army last war? Two days more will be 11 months for me.

It'll be 13 months before I get home in February. Class of 44-5. We graduate 5th week in 1944.

Don't send me anything for Xmas. Save your money. We'll see when I come home. It'll be a piss poor Xmas anyway. No snow, no home, no nothing. Think of me when you drink those Tom & Jerry's.

What's your income tax run? We pay it too, you know. Don't know how much. Not too much.

Got a card from Perry in Tampa, Florida. Mailed Dec 4. Said Nat was getting married nite of Dec 5 by chaplain at Drew Field to Leo Steiner.

Nat's way ahead of Jan in a lot of ways, I guess. She can be ahead of me in that respect. (by 10 years)

Be good now & write.

Love - Your son - Mel xxxxx

Merry Christmas, dad –

Wed-Dec 22, '43 Las Vegas NV

Dear Paw-

Got the 5 spot, and thanx. You asked me what I wanted for Xmas. I guess there's nothing I really need. Mite as well save your money, anyway.

Well, we're deep in the school now, learning leads on enemy planes, etc.

I've learned every part of the machine gun, and can take it apart blindfolded with gloves on in 1 ½ minutes. Pretty good.

Boy! 14 bullets a second. They travel 600 yards in ¾ seconds. Browning was no fool. It's the best gun of its kind in the world. 700 to 850 bullets a minute.

We're really learning to kill our fellow man in earnest now.

I had no effects from the chamber.

Got two cards from the old gal we used to tell stories to in Dewey Jones'. She said to tell you she sent them. There's your chance to go real steady, Romeo.

Also cards from Bid, Moll, & Bessie. And one from a gal in Waseca, Minnesota I don't even know. How come, I wonder?

I'm glad you feel better, Dad. Want you to be o.k., & know you will be.

Save that shoe stamp until I get home, if it's still good there in February. If not, send it along, if you don't really need it. If you do, use it. Don't go without.

I'd rather not have too many medals. Just want to get this war over, and get the hell out of this army soon as I can.

They don't waste any time here. We have Xmas off- but go to school Sunday to make up.

We're in school 10 hours a day now. Quite a grind. Pretty soon we'll be firing, & it won't be too bad then.

Well, old comrade of mine, you be real good. The days are growing short when I'll see ya again, & we'll have some fun. Here's to you, dear old dad, you've got nerve to stick it out all alone, & I love ya for it.

Love- Your son - Mel xxxxx

Sunday, Dec 26 Las Vegas NV

Dear dad -

Now Xmas is but a dim memory-I say dim as there was nothing to mine. I just sat out here, and went to bed about 10:30.

Couldn't even get a brew on the post, & couldn't get into L.V. either.

They're running a concentration camp here. In 7 weeks, you get into town twice, laundry twice, & change of bedding just twice. What the hell kind of a dump have they got here. They've got signs up all over, to wit:

Water is precious, it will be conserved.

It's a wonder they let you take all the showers you want. Funny they don't limit showers to 2 in 7 weeks. Oh hell? I'm disgusted.

For Xmas we had turkey, but there was little or no seasoning in it. But isn't bad.

They had a bad wreck here last nite. Don't know how many were killed in the collision. I know for sure the cab driver, & civilian, owner of the L.V. power & lite & driver of the 42 Buick were killed. Also a Pfc Fred Schmidt of Wisconsin. He's not from around A-F, is he? Also I heard two cadets were killed, & nine more are in the field hospital on the post. Some mixup? The papers didn't mention the A/C's. Maybe they weren't allowed to. The A/C's come here for gunnery between Pre-flite & advanced.

What do they say about a person who writes uphill? A strong personality, or a weak one? It's a lie, & I won't talk till I see my lawyer.

I had booster shots for typhoid and smallpox about an hour ago. The same old story. No effects. Nothing affects me. Except Raaven getting killed at Dalhart, Texas.

We had a test today. Sighting, range estimation, ballistics, aircraft recognition, & the M-2 machine gun. Passed it all, as usual.

This is 3rd week. Four more after this one. Oh boy! Then home. Seems good, hey? They might send us to any kind of a bomber squadron B-26, B-25, B-17G, A-20, or anything. Don't want the B-26. That plane is a death trap. Too short of wings.

The German Focke-Wolf 190 is rated among one of the best planes in the world, & has the best armor plate of any plane in the world. The Jap Zero ("Zeke") has none at all. It blows apart under fire. Among them the P-47 that Ducharme flies in is the best hi-altitude fighter in the world. The P-51 best low-altitude, & the Spitfire of England the best of them all. This doesn't consider the German F6F Hellcat which is still unofficial, but has knocked down all it ran across. It's the only plane that can dog fight a zero, and hope to come out best.

Well, all for now. Love you Dad –

Your son, Mel xxxxx

Tuesday December 28, 1943 Las Vegas NV

Dear Dad -

I'm pretty tired tonite. Got back from Los Angeles this morning at 4:45 A.M. We drove over. Technically, we weren't allowed off the field, but we filled in some blank passes. One kid has a '41 Chevrolet. It was pretty driving over Death Valley early in the morning.

Boulder Dam is only 15 miles S.W. of us. We're going over there soon, too.

Only 2 weeks after this one, & I'll be flying again. That'll be great. I can hardly wait to get into the air again.

We're learning the newest type of sighting, as they've only had it a month now. All the others are obsolete.

We have to learn the length & wingspans of the enemy as we set our automatic computing sights by that.

We were out on the skeet range today. First I ran the automatic buttons that fire the clay birds. Then I only had nine shots, as we had to come eight miles back to the field to go to upper turret drill. Got 6 out of 9.

We use a photo-electric cell (camera gun) to fire in our drill. I got 397 out of 502. Not bad for the 2nd time.

An enemy plane is projected on a big round screen about 30' in diameter, & it looks just like combat conditions.

I was to the Chinese & Hill Street theatres. Also got half stewed up in Ciro's. Their rates are fairly reasonable for service men. Some of the "stars" (hah-hah) were in there, but I don't give a damn for any of them. Phooey on 'em all. That picture industry is a racket.

This is about all I can think of for now.

Still haven't been in Las Vegas. We went thru it, but didn't stop at all on our way to L.A.

Be good, Dad, & take it easy. It's cold here nites, & warm days.

Love - Your son, Mel

TENNESSEE MANEUVERS

Because the Cumberland River area and Tennessee Hills were perceived to be similar to the Rhine and Western Europe, this area was chosen for training the men of the 106th before going overseas. Approximately 20,000 men took part in what they called the Tennessee Maneuvers.

The division left Fort Jackson about the third week in January of 1944. Their trek led them west through Athens, Georgia, the site of their first overnight bivouac. The men anxiously discussed their next stop which was at Fort Oglethorpe. All they could talk about was meeting all of the girls. Fort Oglethorpe was a training center for WACs during the war. Their dreams were not realized as they were restricted to the bivouac area much to their chagrin.

By the time they reached their destination near Murfreesboro, Tennessee, they had covered 442 miles. The weather was balmy, the men basked in sunshine, and it appeared that even though it was January, spring had arrived.

By the end of the month, winter returned with cold rain, sleet and snow. By the middle of February, the temperature was 13 degrees. Clarence certainly remembered the weather when he talked about maneuvers. *"Oh, Tennessee Maneuvers...ha! Don't talk about it. We put water in our helmets to wash our face and the water was freezing! And then we had to try to shave with that ice cold like that.*

"Because I was a driver, I got to ride. Once I got out of South Carolina I never walked anymore. That's why I don't fall asleep when I drive now. I never went to bed. I'd just put my head on the steering wheel and sleep for five minutes and get up again.

"We drove at night all the time, never during the day. We would get bombed otherwise, that was our training. We'd have to put chains on in the Tennessee Hills because of the mud."

Clarence also told me about a man in the division who was from Lebanon, Tennessee. He hated shoes and never wore them. Just plain old couldn't wear them. And apparently no one made him put them on and it was nothing for him to do a twenty-five mile hike barefoot.

The maneuvers lasted seventy-one days and if you read the report, it tells you every move they made while training. It reads like the Intelligence Report during the war. The maneuvers were made up of eight exercises and included bombings, destroying tanks, mustardized demolitions and overtaking rail yards.

Major General Alan W. Jones commanded the Red Force (which Clarence was a part of) during the sixth exercise. He was with the men in the Schnee Eifel. To this day, when Clarence goes to the VA Clinic, he is still considered part of the 'red team.'

GUNNERY SCHOOL

There were 27 killed in one day at Kingman Arizona gunnery school, 100 miles from here. Cheerful?

January 8, 1944 Las Vegas NV

Dear dad-

Haven't written for a few days, so guess I'll catch up.

A week ago I saw a guy lose $35,000 at the El Rancho Vegas. It's a big gambling joint 2 miles out of L.V. They broadcast from there, have all sorts of liquor and floor shows.

I was there again last nite and played a little. Won $5.00 playing at $2 a time. Next to the Last Frontier, I guess it's the biggest joint in the country.

Stopped into the Last Frontier last nite and Hedy Lamar was there. Sophie Tucker got up & sang a couple and pulled dirty jokes. She's no good for my money.

A week from today, we start to fly. Get flying clothes this week. Oxygen masks, parachutes.

We're the horned toads of Las Vegas, as you can see on the matches.

We shot from the back of trucks yesterday. My ears still ring. Day before we shot 12 gauge shotguns mounted in turrets. Imagine that. I always do pretty good. You know, I'll make a good hunter. Especially ducks. My accuracy is improving. You'd be surprised how they can make a good shot out of you. They spend a lot of money on you here.

Three weeks left. Oh boy!

Thirteen guys bailed out six days ago, and two of them are still missing.

I've been busier than hell. 10 -11 hours of school & shooting a day. It's fun though.

Talked to a top turret gunner from Guadalcanal. Fifty three missions and only one bullet had hit the plane. It came into the turret and hit the sight. Ruined it but saved his life.

Then, on their 54th and last mission, a 20 mm cannon shell hit it and blew the plane in two & killed both waist gunners.

I see several guys that have D.F.C. And others have air medals, & silver stars. I don't give a damn for the medals if I can come back in one piece, with the war over, and civilian life waiting for me. I mean it.

Well, I'll write again soon, comrade, & be good. I'll see ya' in less than a month.

Love,

Your son, Mel

January 17, 1944 Indian Springs Nev.

Dear dad-

Well, here I am at Indian Springs for a week of flying. I wrote you a letter 2 days ago. I can't find out if I mailed it or not. Can't find it, & don't remember dropping it in the box.

Today makes a year of army. At 3:30 I got on the train and I remember we hit that car south of Racine and killed two people.

Well, we drew $500.00 worth of equipment - winter helmet & goggles, summer helmet & oxygen mask, boots, pants, & winter jackets, two kit bags, chest parachute & harness, gloves, and "Mae West" life vest. We'll still have lots to draw.

Two weeks from today, we graduate. Then I lay around till that Wednesday, and when the shipping orders come thru, I'm off for Wisconsin. You see, this isn't a regular furlough, it's a delay on the way to the next field where we're made into crews in bombers.

Matlock took his first ride this morning at 7 A.M. Still gone yet. Hope he's ok. I loaned him my jacket, as the tail end guys didn't get all their stuff.

His sister wrote me, and asked me, among other things, if I bit my fingernails. I said "Hell yes, and if I'm in another year, I'll be biting my toenails too, so don't think anything of it, kid!"

Matlock came back ok a few minutes ago. I was afraid he'd get paint on it from the bullets. They're dipped in paint on the tips so they can tell who hit's the target.

I fly high altitude tomorrow morning. Over 18,000 feet. We fire at a sleeve towed by another plane with the waist guns.

Then we fire the chin turret in the bombardier's nose and the upper turret at another sleeve. We fire the chin turret at an outline of a ship on the ground. Just practice & no score is kept.

We fly the latest B-17G. The only one that has the chin turret is the "G". This is the plane we'll use at O.T.V. next, and overseas. We have to fix every position, and believe me leads & lags are different on everyone. Even the ball turret.

We go back to the L.V. field next Sunday for a final week of camera guns.

A lot of the guys are routed right through Chicago to South Carolina & Florida. At that rate, it will only cost me from Chicago to Adams round trip. I'd like to go to the East Coast. Never been to North Carolina, South Carolina, Georgia or Florida. I'd probably hit 'em all if I got assigned to Tampa Florida.

Matlock came in and gave me a box of stationary his sister sent him for me. She's 24 years old and witty as hell. She swears like a pirate in letters to him, but doesn't say anything in mine. Give her time, I say. That makes 3 girls I write to I've never seen, and probably never will. One in Waseca Minnesota & two in Philadelphia.

I guess quite a few of the guys got airsick. Christ, if they get sick on these, what would they do on those Beechcraft AT- 7's we had at Monroe Louisiana.

We go up in the morning. Fire upper turrets in air to air and the chin turrets in air to ground.

I have to take that back about the chin turrets.

They are already obsolete, and the B-17H is made without it.

Well, this is about all I can think of for now. So you be good, and I'll see ya' in the near future.

Love,

Your son- Mel xxxxx

January 19, 1944 Las Vegas NV

Dear dad -

We flew yesterday morning, & we were over Death Valley Calif.

The mountains look funny. No growth on them.

I fired the flexible gun on the left side & shot 410 times.

A B-26 dragged a sleeve back and forth across us over & under. That's a fast plane, 380 M.P.H.

The ball turret fired twin 50 cal. The floor would jump every time he opened up.

Then we came down, and fired at silhouettes of planes on the ground tearing by at 500 feet.

I was putting them thru the target fairly well. I fired the .30 cal.

We were up 4 hours. Only one guy got sick, & he threw up all over. He was up forward though, and I never knew it.

We didn't see Boulder Dam, but will later on.

All for now. Be good.

Love, comrade

Your Son - Mel xxxxx

January 19, 1944 Las Vegas, NV

Dear Dad -

I'll be 23 tomorrow. But that doesn't mean anything.

So Neuman is in Gulfport. Our train backed into there once on our way from Keesler to Amarillo.

I imagine the guy that lost the $35,000 was rich, but I hadn't been out for a long time, and didn't pay much attention to him.

Dunham wrote and said his outfit was going overseas either January 15th or 20th. So he must be in that bunch. He sure spent enuf time in North Carolina.

We graduate the 31st of January and get going February 2nd or 3rd.

The leaves are automatic. Everyone gets them.

Got the birthday card, thanks.

I sure have got a hell of a cold. Had it before I got to Indian Springs, tho, & it hasn't gotten worse, even if we are in tents. Nothing up here is good. I'll be glad when I get out of here Sunday.

Did you get the match folder? Hope so.

All for now.

Love - Your Son - Mel xxxxx

January 24, 1944 Las Vegas, NV

Dear Dad -

We'll leave Wednesday, the 2nd. Graduate on the 31st, a week from today.

If I'd get sent to the East Coast, and routed through Chicago, as lots have, it would cost me only from Chicago to Adams. Sure hope that happens. Never been on the East Coast.

They called us in and had us fill out a form asking us if we wanted to be instructors.

I said absolutely not.

They send the future instructors to Fort Myers, Fla. for four weeks. Give you advanced machine gun, and courses in teaching. Must have at least a H.S. education, and a CTCT of 120 or better. I've got all qualifications except the desire.

Just the fact that I said I didn't want it, doesn't mean I won't get it. Just means I probably won't get it. Sure hope I don't.

Funny thing, when they send them back to teach, they'll send them any place in the USA except the one where they were trained. You tell me how the army works.

Only three more flights. We're all through firing. It's all camera now. A double check on our shooting, I 'spose. The camera tells the story.

Love to you,

Your son, Mel xxxxx

Be good, and I'll be seeing you shortly.

January 28, 1944 Las Vegas, NV

Dear dad -

Well, I'll leave the 2nd, and be home at 3:30 A.M. of the 5th. Morning 400, of course. That isn't for sure. But I'll be there then, or else on the 400 the 4th. So you can't lose.

I'd like you to see the flying clothes I've got, but don't know if I can bring them or not. We'll see.

This'll probably be the last letter I'm going to write unless something turns up.

I was scheduled to go to B-26 at Shreveport, La, but Matlock & McTavey are going to Columbia, S.C., & I got the Lieutenant to change mine to there. I heard they had B-25's there. But don't know for sure. Besides, I've been in Shreveport before, and flew over it, but never have been in S.C.

Matlock's sister sent me the paper I'm writing on, & also some cakes, & candy for Jan. 20. Mat must have told her, wrote & thanked her. Write her steady anyway.

Gotta write Dunham too. Been a long time again. Also Kenyon. Never heard from Rigdon. Cuss him.

We have ten full days at home. Not long enuf. Plus travel time.

All for now. Be good. I'll be seeing ya, bud.

Your son-Mel xxxxx

The '400' that Melvin is referring to is the passenger train that ran from Chicago to Minneapolis St. Paul, stopping in Adams. It was 400 miles and 400 minutes between the cities.

Melvin did get a ten day furlough and him and Grandpa must have had a few drinks his last night home. He writes again after getting settled in Columbia, South Carolina, and mentions the 'Beanery' in his letter.

Interestingly, in the contents of the boxes, there was a postcard with the '400' on it and a newspaper which had an ad for the Beanery which apparently was one of the happening places at the time.

B25'S

Dear dad-

I finally arrived here on the field at 8:30 at nite on the 18th, a day late. They didn't say anything, as I missed connections in Cincinnati, Ohio. They had a wreck up the line, and we went 100 miles out of our way.

Adams to Chg. 4 hrs; to Cincy 10 ½ hrs; to Atlanta, Ga 14 hrs; to Spartenburg S.C. 5 hrs; to Columbia 4 ½ hrs. 37 ½ hrs. Long enuf to get here.

They've got A-20 & B-25 planes here. Guess I'll get a B-25. Don't care one way or the other.

Was really swell when we got here. 85 degrees F. But it has rained almost ever since. At least they've got trees here.

It's 7 miles from the base to the town. They've got Fort Jackson over on the other side, also 7 miles out. I hear it's a really big post. One of the biggest in the USA.

They don't let those birds in, only on weekends. We get in whenever we want to. Got it all over them.

Columbia is the capital. About 100,000 people. Not a bad place. State building is a dome, but a lot smaller than at Madison. And not half as pretty.

Wrote you from Atlanta. Hope you get it.

Tennessee had a lot of flood waters. Must've rained plenty there.

Added 3 more states to my collection. Ga, Ohio, & S.C. Twenty-seven now. Not bad. Twenty-one to go.

We must've been at the top of our lungs in the Beanery. I was sure in sad shape when I got in Chicago. Hangover. Didn't even eat breakfast at all.

It doesn't seem like I was home at all, now that I've gotten back into the army way. Guess that's life for ya', huh?

Don't believe I'll ever be stoic & calm until the war is over & I can throw these clothes away. I just can't wait.

More later, going to a show now, & then bed.

Love - Your Son - Mel xxxxx

Be good, paw!

I guess rivalry is always healthy. That's what I'm told anyhow. Melvin sure had something to say about being one up on the Fort Jackson guys. And in the past, I can still hear Clarence saying how easy the Army Air Corps guys had it.

Melvin had commented, too, on how much rain Tennessee must have had. Clarence could attest to that fact. As he was wallowing in the mud, the train Melvin was on no doubt passed him by on his way to Columbia.

Feb 24, 1944 Columbia SC

Dear dad -

Well, not too much to say. Don't know where I'm at yet. They said we're here from 8 to 15 days yet.

Still no flying. Not 'til we hit O.I.U. This is a replacement depot. I won't draw flying pay 'til next month.

I've had shots for cholera, of which there is two more, & a booster for tetanus. Also one typhus. Took all three at once in one arm. It wasn't half as sore as I figured.

I've managed to get me another cold, but not a hard one.

I'm sending you a power of atty. We also have to make a will when we go overseas. That's ok too. I made Molly my next in line on the $10,000 insurance. In case you were gone. We'll never argue about it if she collects, hey? So what's the difference?

I might get assigned here, Greensboro, Charlotte, or Spartanburg. Don't care a damn. It'll be A-20, or B-25. All for now.

Love, Your son - Mel xxxxx

I'll send that power of atty. You can transfer that $11.00 to your acct, then, I guess.

Love, Mel

March 1, 1944

Dear dad -

Went in the pressure chamber for 1 ¼ hours this morn. Went to 25,000' without oxygen. Last one in ten to put on my mask.

He had me subtracting, writing "Mary had a little lamb", my name, serial no., rank, home address, etc. Finally, my brain still worked, but I wrote all over the page. Just couldn't make my hand do what I wanted. Funniest feeling I ever had. Like a drunken man. But I knew what I was doing, and I don't think a drunk does, do you? Funny, but at the time, a person still thinks he's alright. No sense of danger. That's the real danger of anopia. A person can die up there without even realizing he's in danger. He told me to put my mask on. A few breaths of oxygen, and I realized how bad off I'd been.

Then we turned out all the lights, and you could barely see the phosphorus hands of the altimeter. Then we turned 'em on and put on red polaroid glasses ($36.00 each) for ten minutes. Then turned the lights off. I could read altitude, and see everyone in there. Then we put our hands over one eye and turned them on again. Exposed one eye for ten minutes. Then turned 'em off. First used one eye, and then the other. Just like being blind in one eye.

Never a dull moment in the Army Air Corps.

I am now assigned for the first time. To the 3rd Air Force. Here's the shoulder patch. And also the mechanic patch I could wear on my right sleeve 4" from the cuff, but don't. That's a radical engine by the way. Notice that classy new address? Swear I was somebody.

I got a new Waterman's 8.75 pen at the P.X. tonite. Only 5.00, too. Everything is cheaper.

We just moved across the field. I lost Matlock. He's over there. But I've still got McTavey. He & I are the only ones left of the famous five of Amarillo whose pictures I sent you. Now we get our crews. I heard we don't get to fly for 6 weeks yet. But also heard we get in one flight to get our flight pay for this month. 99.00 instead of 66.00. Ok by me. 33.00 ain't hay.

I guess engineers get S/Sgt. before they go overseas. Hope so. 96.00 x 1 ½ =144.00 + 20% = $163.20. Not bad.

I should have a good 3 months yet. We might get to Madison. It's only 1100 miles. About three hours by air. Amazing, hey? But we're in B-25's, and they're really fast. No kidding.

Met a kid here I knew in Monroe, La. Andy Rodrigues from Witt, Illinois. He's a 2nd Lt. Got bombardier after he washed out of nav. He admits he was lucky at getting it.

I'm going to draw my summer flying clothes tomorrow. A guy told us today that an airman draws more stuff than any other man in uniform. I sure don't doubt it.

Well, guess I've wrote all the news, & now you're up to date again.

Hope to hear from you.

Your Son - Love - Mel xxxxx x5 25-x's Right?

March 2, 1944

Dear dad -

I'm sending you a new power of atty. The other one is no good. It isn't notarized. Also a will we had to make.

Just a note now, as I just wrote you a big letter.

Figured I've had 15 shots so far. Only one left. 3rd typhus. Had a yellow fever shot today. Reminds me of a pin cushion.

4 tetanus, 2 cholera, 4 typhoid, 2 typhus (one to go),
1 yellow fever, 2 smallpox – 15 - not bad?

All for now,

Love, Your Son, Mel xxxxx

March 8, 1944

Dear dad -

Here is the will & a new P. of A. The other one might
be ok. I don't know. One of those copies should have
been left here with the army. You can tear it up, as
this one is ok for sure.

Well, we have a week of aircraft engineering & three
weeks of armament, being as how there are Bendix
turrets, and the B-17-G's at L.V. were Sperry.

My stomach has been upset today. Nothing serious.
Just a loss of appetite, & all.

Hope you're ok. You go on the blink like that every
once in a while.

I have a pilot from New York City, a Chinese Nav -
cannoneer from L.A. Calif, & don't know where the
radio-gunner and armorer-gunner are from.

The Chink had 7 weeks nav, and a full bombardier's course. I had more nav. than he did. He's also

a cannoneer as we'll carry the 75 m.m. in the nose. Also will do skip bombing.

In 3 ½ weeks we go to Myrtle Beach for a week of advanced gunnery. Then back here and we start flying with our one crew all the time for the last 8 weeks. Then we'll go to the P.O.E. (Port of Embarkation) which is in Savannah, Georgia for this neck of the woods. There we'll lay around from 6 days to 6 weeks waiting out all of our final checks, and a brand new airplane, which we'll fly overseas. With the aid of a group navigator, of course. One who can do celestial nav. and get us there for sure.

Well, Matlock is at Charlotte, N.C. with an A-20 squadron. Had a letter from him already and answered it. Right prompt of he and I both, don't you think?

I'm running all out of thoughts now.

One of the nav-can's lost his head today, and bailed out when a motor quit cold on them. It was a chest 'chute, and the lines cut hell out of his face 'cause he failed to throw his arm up to his face. What a dope! Those lines can knock your teeth out. That much power. Well, he's got time to think it all over in the hospital now.

All for now –

Love from your son, Mel xxxxx

March 18, 1945 Columbia SC

Dear Dad,

Well, I got the watch & it is still running ok. So I guess it's fixed all right this time.

You said you didn't think 25.00 insurance covered it. I don't think so either. 40.00 is more like it. Tell Harry many thanx.

Well, I was up to Charlotte, N.C. to see Matlock Sat. and Sun. McTavey & I went all over Morris Field, and up to the flight line to see the A-20's. Nice plane, but I sure wouldn't swap the B-25 for them. Another state for my collection.

I thought that pic was pretty good too. I'll try & have some made in flying duds if I can get some 627 film. I think that a kid has a camera here I can borrow.

Well, Mom was 43 the 17th. St. Patrick's. She should still have 20-30 yrs left instead of 2 ½ yrs gone. The mockery of life!

You and I have been closer than we ever were before I got in uniform, you know. Guess it's just since Mom died.

Charlotte is only 102 miles from here. The town is a lot better than Columbia.

We're on flying status now since yesterday. All we need now is the hours in the air. We'll get them next month. And we can back up on our hours, and collect for Feb. & March also. $66.00 more. Nice.

Have to get my summer flying clothes some nite now. I've got my vital area pass to the warehouses and flight line now.

All for now, comrade. See ya later -

Be good dad, old pal

Love - your son - Mel xxxxx

March 30, 1944 Columbia SC

Dear dad -

Well, Sunday we go down to the shore at Myrtle Beach, S.C. for 10 days.

Got a card from Frank Hladilek. 'Spose you did too. He has a kid. Named it Charles Earl born March 11th, 5 pounds 4 oz at St. Mary's.

Will drop him a line & call him pop. He'll get a bang out of that. Christ, he's sure as hell made himself a bed to sleep in now, hey? Glad it ain't me. I'd rather be in the army than that. Much as I hate this deal.

We go out on the skeet range tomorrow. More shotguns. Ho hum!

Had another ride in an A-20 Sunday. What a plane. 370 M.P.H. Was up to Charlotte again.

Matlock's wife comes in this week. Quit a 180.00 a month job selling R.R. tickets in the Penn. Station to come down. Ain't love horrible?

How's ole Wis? No monthly report from you lately.

All for now.

Love to ya, dad,

Your best son, Mel xxxxx

April 3, 1944 Columbia SC

Dear Comrade -

Well, here I am at the Beach. I can see the ocean from the field.

We've got better barracks here than back at the other field. Every day it rains here is a lost day. You have to put in seven flights before you go back to CAAB.

I'm kind of glad I got out of navigation now. On Dec 7 when I was at Las Vegas I wrote two of my friends who were ready to go to England as navigators on B-17s.

Both letters came back stamped "missing in action". I'll send you the envelopes when I get back to the other base. Plenty of stamps on them.

We came down by truck convoy yest. 162 miles. They gave us 4.00 to eat on to & fro. We stopped in Florence for dinner. Had a big steak for 1.25.

It's raining now. What a miserable mess. We've got trees all around us. Just like we were out in the wilds, which in truth we are, I guess.

Had a letter from Fannie Straus. Asked me if they could do anything for you. She said you appear blue and downhearted over half the time. Told me to write her, and I will.

Was over to the alleys last nite here, and bowled 3 games 135, 139, 156. 15 cents a line. Can't spend too much money. Pretty short. Don't send me none. I don't need it. Just got to take it easy.

I haven't gotten you a thing for your birthday yet, but I'll make it up to you, wait & see.

Not much other news, so I'll close now.

An A-20 roared over us by 20 feet yesterday, as we came here by truck.

Well, old dad of mine, Be good, and I will, too. Xxxxx

Love -your son, Mel

4-12-44

Dear dad -

I guess I'm way in the rear on this letter business.
I'm sorry, so here goes. I'm back from Myrtle Beach,
& out on the line pulling pre-flite inspections on
planes. We have a week of that.

Kind of a dead week. Could've gotten a three day
pass, but had no dough to spend lavishly, so turned
it down. Don't especially care, either.

Lewis said Hamilton was broken to a Pvt. Was a Cpl.
It's his rugged spirit.

Got 3 hrs 10 min. Need 50 minutes more for this
month. Guess I'll get it sooner or later in the month.
Hope so. Won't for a couple of weeks anyhow. Can't
write worth a damn tonite.

See if you can get some 127 film. I can't. Got all my
flying clothes.

Been hot here. Cold in the morning. Miserable goddamn state.

Rigdon dropped me a card from Fresno, Calif. He got
married. Hell's bells.

Can't write tonite at all. So what? I say - - -

Saw a demonstration on incendiary bombs tonite. A B-25 dropped clusters of them 100 yds from us.

I haven't written anyone for a week or better. Just have been so disrupted, and have had such ridiculous hours that I've been tired all the time lately. I'll do better again now.

We sure are sending the guys out of here overseas every day, just between you and me. I must have 7 or 8 weeks left yet.

How about Capt. Bong from Poplar, Wisc? 27 enemy planes. Leading ace in the Pacific—

One guy from Ohio has 30 but 7 were destroyed on the ground and you don't count those on the ground. Well, I'm going to close for tonite, as I'm tired. I was painting numbers on ships all day today.

Love, Your son Mel, xxxxx

P.S. Here are those 2 envelopes. Prout was one of my best friends. I saw the other one, Palmer, in Amarillo. His went to Dalhort, Texas, Grand Island, Nebraska, A.P.O.-N.Y.C., England, Las Vegas, and here. Prout's, Longbranch, N.J.-A.P.O.-N.Y.C. England, Las Vegas, and here. Both are stamped, or written, Missing in Action.

I have learned so much not only from Clarence, but from Melvin's letters. When a name or place is mentioned that I have never heard of, I dig in and see what else I have missed. Which of course, is a lot. This time, since I had never heard of Captain Richard Ira Bong from Poplar, Wisconsin, I decided to find out more.

One of the returned envelopes marked 'Missing in Action'

When Melvin wrote this letter, his numbers for Major Bong were accurate. By the end of his time overseas, he was credited with forty planes being shot down. When he came home, he married his sweetheart, Marge, who's picture was on his plane. They were married on February 10, 1945 and Major Bong became a test pilot assigned to Lockheed's plant in Burbank, California. On August 6, 1945, due to a malfunction of the primary fuel pump, the P80A he was flying crashed in a field in North Hollywood.

There is a Richard I. Bong Veterans Historical Center in Superior, Wisconsin, that I will be visiting the first chance I get. There are other tributes to him such as a bridge, recreational area, an airport and even a theater in Japan named after him. He was indeed a hero. But then, they all were.

May 8, 1944 Columbia SC

Dear dad -

Well I had a clothing check today. Anything that has a little tear or frayed edge on it, they give you brand new.

We also have to have microphones sewn in our helmets, and our "Mae West's" inspected

We draw pistol belts, etc. Draw a .45 at Savannah, Ga. P.O.E. (Port of Embarkation)

Tomorrow the whole crew has a physical exam. We haven't got long left in the U.S.A. 3-4 weeks, I'd say.

We're in the air day & nite lately. Don't know if I'll even have a chance to learn my 2nd degree the way they're rushing us. There's an invasion coming, and they're stepping it up to beat hell.

I'll probably see you the 13th. I'll ride up as tail gunner. Barring bad weather and all, of course. I'll know tomorrow.

Got 50 hours in the air here. Still going strong.

Flew a formation today. Rough as hell.

A guy just gave me a drink of whiskey. Warmed me to the boiling point. Damn!

No accidents lately. Keeping my fingers crossed.

It's hot here today. Or else it's my imagination. Could be.

I'm going to New York City the 27th also. With my own crew as engineer.

I was up in the top turret training my guns and ship nearest me in the formation.

I've got a class in the morning, so no sleep for the wicked. Everything comes at once. Fly tonite too.

All for now. Love to ya -dad,

Your son - Mel xxxxx

May 11, 1944 Columbia SC

Dear dad -

Well, I have news for you, old bean.

I'm leaving here tonite for Warrensburg, Mo. Ferry Command. Everyday we're away from home base, we get 7.00 a day maintenance for hotel bills & food. Best deal in the air corps.

Columbia, South Carolina, Melvin, ?, ?, McTavey, ? and ?

They made me Sgt. today also. Heh-heh.

We'll ferry ships all over the country. Also may be paratroopers in the S. Pacific. What a deal! Travel all the time. 210.00 month for maintenance. Plus flight pay. Boy!!

We got 7.00 today for meals plus a Pullman from Atlanta to St. Louis.

Was in Tallahassee Fla yesterday. 1 ½ hours to fly there. That B-25 really gets out and goes. Went to Birmingham, Ala the other nite. Also Myrtle Beach & Atlanta.

We'll be 65 miles out of Kansas City, Mo.

You never know how the army operates. No trip to Chgo now. And I was looking forward to seeing ya', too, dad. But maybe I will later, we'll see.

I've got to pack, so I'll close this off for now, and write you as soon as I get there.

Love to ya, dad

Your son - Mel xxxxx

WHY AM I HERE ?

May 19, 1944 Warrensburg, MO

Dear dad -

I held off writing a little bit hoping I could tell you what I'm doing here, but I can't. They sent a letter back about us to try and find out. Nobody seems to know on the whole field. We're the only 12 gunners here. And the planes (C-47) don't carry guns. They told us the whole thing was a mistake, and we wouldn't be here too long. Hope not.

I'd take a discharge if I could get one now. Hell's bells! They don't even want me to fight!! That's been proven to me on this last little deal.

I would have been already for overseas by the first of the month.

Love to ya, dad –

Your "best" son - Mel xxxxx

Dear dad - Monday Warrensburg MO

I guess it's about time I wrote you again.

I was going to come up Saturday, but all the planes were full up. So I went to Kansas City yesterday AM. Stayed overnite. The guy I was with had his billfold stolen. Didn't have enuf money in it to amount to a damn, but a lot of important papers.

The fellow we rode back with today was on his way to Hot Springs, Ark. I drove all the way from K.C. to here.

I'm hoping to come up to Milw. next Sat. Think I can, too.

I wish I knew how long we'll be here. Nothing more has been heard since the last time. When the trans-fers came back, I mean.

This place gets on my nerves, and I don't mean perhaps.

Yesterday was Father's Day. I didn't send you any-thing as I didn't know of anything you really need, except a blonde and a million dollars.

I'll fly from 5 PM this afternoon to 2 AM in the morn-ing. Nine hours. It's already 3:45. Must close this soon, and get over to eat, and get ready.

They still haven't gotten our flying pay settled. That one month I have got coming has yet to come in from Columbia. Also that bastard down there didn't send my laundry. Cuss his ornery hide. On top of that, their flying pay is always 1 month behind times, so all I can draw the first of July, providing I'm here and on the payroll is 10 days for May. We shipped out on the 11th, you know?

We go to a place in K.C. called "Plamor". Swimming pools, dance floor, bowling, tennis, etc. Really big. Covers a square block.

All for now, dad –

Love, Your son - Mel xxxxx

July 19, 1944 Tampa FL

Dear Pop -

Told you I'd drop you a line when I got to Chgo. Here 'tis.

Nothing much to tell. It's now 10AM. Four more hours to go.

Setting here in the USO that's supposed to be the best in the U.S.A. Plenty good.

I dread that 41 hour ride, but guess it's all in the interest of democracy, so what the hell.

All for now, pop.

Love - Your "best" son - Mel xxxxx

July 22, 1944 Tampa FL

Dear dad -

Arrived here at 2 PM in the afternoon of the 21st.

Plant Park is right in the heart of Tampa. Guess it used to be a baseball park. We live in the stadium as there's more of us, and the Lts. live in tents. It's about the same anyway.

I got off the Limited at Albany, Ga. as it was 2 ½ hours late and I'd never made connections at Jacksonville at 11PM the 20th. Stayed at Albany for 7 ½ hours. Went to a dance after I'd shaved, showered, and changed clothes.

I haven't been into Tampa as yet as I don't have a helluva lot of money.

I'd figured that check for those pants and shirts had come, but guess it hasn't.

I've got to buy me some cigs, soap, and a toothbrush, and I'll be about broke again.

Will get our travel pay in a week or two, they said. Probably two, if I know this place.

The trip down was pretty uneventful. I got here a day late and Olliff & a kid were behind me. Olliff got here an hour after I did. The other one isn't even here yet. Two days late now.

One of our guys went out on the nite of the 20th and ended up in the guard house dead drunk with a big tattoo on his left forearm.

I've got to wash and shave again today. Every day I shave now.

A while ago the sun was shining, and now it's raining to beat hell. Sunny Florida. I've seen 'em all in the South for sure now, and what I said still goes.

McTavey said he'd send my stuff down here or wherever I went to as soon as he heard from me. Said it'd been lost but he'd traced it and gotten it back.

Most of the guys I knew in Columbia are in Hawaii. Guess I'd be there too, if I'd stayed in S.C.

Don't make any difference to me, tho. This is all B-17 Flying Fortress's here.

Love,

Your son, Mel xxxxx

July 31, 1944 Tampa FL

Dear dad -

Well, I heard tonite we were going to Shreveport La. for the B-26.

McTavey went over. Opposite direction from Matlock. We sure got split up.

Tampa isn't such a wonderful place. This Hillsborough Hotel isn't too bad. They've got an air conditioned bar downstairs. Not bad.

Well, I'm on my 19th month now. A real veteran.

I guess I never will get overseas. At least it looks like it.

Well, I started this letter last nite, and I'll finish it now. It's just as well as I have more news now.

I'm being shipped back to Columbia, S.C. We're going into the B-25 again. We were alerted today, and should go tomorrow. Well, I'll finish this now, and go and pack. You can write here, as all our mail for this afternoon was already forwarded to Col. They really spent the taxpayer's money foolishly this time, eh?

Love, as ever –

Your son, Mel xxxxx

V-MAIL

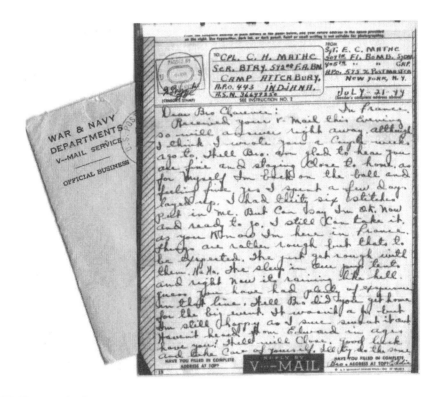

Clarence received several v-mail letters, better known as victory letters. This became a secure method for soldiers to correspond during
the war. Once the letters were censored, they were copied on to microfilm, sent to their destination, and then the negatives would be blown up,

printed and delivered. This saved shipping space for more important war materials.

Most of the letters Clarence received were from his brother Edmund, but he also received a few from his old buddy Harold. Him and Harold were friends from way back and had actually helped Lucille pop the cork on the champagne bottle when she was a mere sixteen years old.

For all of the memorabilia I have of Melvin's, and even though he mentions v-mail letters, I have yet to find any.

One of the popular words of the era must have been 'swell.' It was used often by both Edmund and Harold and by now it has been noticed in some of Melvin's letters, also. What another *swell* part of history for us to remember.

KEE—RIST IT'S HOT HERE!

August 4, 1944 Columbia SC

Dear dad -

Here I am, back in the replacement depot right where I was last February, except for two things. I'm a sgt instead of a cpl and a little bit wiser.

Sure is plenty hot here. And I mean really boiling hot.

I changed my 2nd beneficiary to Gram today.

We had pullmans on the way up. For the first time I enjoyed a train ride in the army.

They're trying to screw me on the flight pay. It'll be a loss of 39.00 to me if they do. I have to write back to Mo. & see if they'll realize their mistake. Hope so! Also I have ten days in May to diddle with. Plus this month's pay.

All for now.

Love - Your best son, Mel xxxxx

August 10, 1944 Columbia SC

Dear dad -

Sitting here smoking a White Owl cigar. Guess I'll get this letter off before I go into town.

No flight pay yet. Should be able to draw some this month if I can get to flying.

We're going over to the Bomb Crew section tomorrow to start R.T.U. all over again. Right back where I was 4 months ago.

I'll use our address over there altho I'll be here 'til tomorrow.

Here's part payment on all that money you gave me. More when I get it. Guess I'll buy a pair of shoes also.

Let me know when you get this money order.

This mail situation is the nuts. None of my mail from Tampa is coming at all.

I've heard from you once since I came back from Adams. Maybe you're sick?

Well, I'll write again soon, dad & let you know more. There's nothing here in the depot to tell. Just had a physical & passed, of course.

Well, love to ya', dad old boy.

Love - From your son, Mel xxxxx

August 15, 1944 Columbia SC

Dear dad -

Found out today we'll be getting a leave to come home while the rest of our crews are going thru this ground school.

We went thru it once before, so skip it this time.

Those pictures weren't bad. I looked heavier than Dunham in those pics. You looked pretty good in those at the fair. A little tanked, but what the hell.

All for now, but more later, of course.

Love From your "best" sonny to my "best" dad,

Mel xxxxx

Obviously he did get his furlough and they had a great time. This is a picture of Melvin, Bob Dunham and my grandpa, Manley. Maybe it's about time you could put a face to the person receiving all of these letters. I will write more about Bob Dunham later.

Bob Dunham, Manley Pollock, Melvin Pollock

August 30, 1944 (post card stamped in Chicago)

Dear Dad:

Seems like a long time since I left. Only last nite, tho. Will write another in Cinncy if I have time. Should anyway.

Love - Best son, Mel xx

September 2, 1944 Columbia SC

Dear dad -

I guess it's about time I wrote and told you I'm alive.

I got here at 7:00 P.M. on the 31st. Dirty as hell, & tired. Those Southern trains are a helluva lot dirtier than the ones up there.

Our crews haven't finished ground school yet. This is another guy's pen. He's using mine. Wants a left hander to break it in for him. Scratches to beat hell.

They'll have Myrtle Beach coming up & we'll skip that also.

Right now we're not doing a damn thing. Could have still been home. Would sure like to have been yet.

Got potted up good last nite. Six of us. Every one of us got potted up. Had 2 qts. of blended bourbon, and a lot of beer.

I heard from McTavey. He's in Corsica and has made 2 missions into south France. Says it isn't bad at all. Dropped a lot of bombs both trips. Matlock has seen several of the boys from here as they come into New Guinea.

There isn't much news. Nothing has happened here. We're not flying at all. Darn near flew to Vermont, but another guy who lived up there wanted to go. Don't blame him.

The Kee birds sit on top of the telephone poles & holler "Kee-rist!! It's hot up here!!"

Well, all for now. Ran out of steam now. Nothing really to write about anyway.

Love From your "best" son –

Mel xxxxx

September 6, 1944 Columbia SC

Dear Dad -

Guess it's about time I wrote you another letter. Just haven't had time, it seems like. That's a poor excuse, isn't it? But it's the only one I have.

Nothing has happened. We haven't flown yet. All the squadrons have been filled up with training crews, & no room for passengers trying to get time in.

We just sleep till 11 o'clock every morning, & sit up half the nite playing cards & checkers. That's since last nite. Tonite I'll get caught up on some of my letters.

Guess what. I'm raising a beautiful mustache. Five days now, & you can see it pretty good. After I get it all grown, I'll have some 10 cent pictures taken, & send 'em along. Whewwwww!! Oh, they'll be beauties, I tell ya. Heh - heh!

Saw Abbot & Costello this A.M. & they weren't too bad. We'd been down to the line to fly, but they were full to the brim. So we went to the cinema.

We haven't done a damn thing since we've been back. Could've still been home.

This place gripes me. Wonder how the infantry guys keep from going crazy. They lead a deader existence than even we do now.

Went in town & got a good steak last nite. Then we watched the "Angel" wrestle. It was lousy. All faked, and not even good.

All for now,

Love - Your "best" son Mel xxxxx

September 10, 1944 Columbia SC midnite

Dear Paw,

Haven't heard from you for a few days now, Pop. Are you all ok? I hope.

We searched till four o'clock this morning for a crash. It was found while we were re-fueling. All six were dead. Got to bed at eight this morning. Couldn't sleep because all the boys were packing to go to Myrtle Beach for that week of gunnery. We didn't have to go because we'd already had it before, remember?

Saw Carmen Miranda & Don Ameche in a show tonite. Wasn't so hot. Not interesting enuf.

I just got up at six tonite, and now I'm going back to bed as soon as I finish this letter. Got up just in time to get a few cold sandwiches over at the mess hall. And then the weather was damp and miserable tonite to boot. My spirits are all wet tonite, anyhow.

I heard Dick Neuman was home. Guess he might still be there?

Love to my "best" Dad:

Your "best" Son, Mel xxxxx

September 13, 1944 Columbia SC

Dearest dad -

The days are really slipping along, and here I am, still playing extra board, as the R.R. men would say. Ok by me, tho.

We've been having some rough flying weather lately. That's why those boys cracked up the other nite, they said. Hit an air pocket while hedgehopping. Now I learn it's because of a general storm condition which has developed into a hurricane off Florida and is heading for here. Let her come. More fun.

Sat up about half the nite listening to big bands all over the country before I got sleepy.

Really have been living like a big time operator. You know, the kind that run all nite & sleep all day.

Tell Charlie Cavanaugh each 24 hours brings me closer to that quart of Scotch. I really think I'll win now. Germany will fite to the last ditch. Revolution will beat them.

I wish those lousy bastards who call themselves human beings would quit, as I'm sick of pissing my young life away in this goddamn neck of the woods.

If I feel like it, I'll start flying with my pilot. The rest aren't back from Myrtle Beach, and won't be if this hurricane business keeps up. He's scheduled for tomorrow morning, but I won't get up. So I'll get at it tomorrow nite.

Don't feel like writing letters or anything else. Guess this army is ruining me, but good.

The 12 bottles

I had 12 bottles of whiskey in the cellar and my wife told me to empty them down the sink, - or else —

So, I withdrew the cork from the first bottle and poured it down the sink, with the exception of one glass, which I drank. I extracted the cork form the 2nd bottle and did likewise, with the exception of one glass, which I drank. I withdrew the cork from the 3rd glass and poured the whiskey down the sink, with the exception of the bottle I drank. I pulled the cork from the 4th sink and poured the bottle down the glass, which I drank. I pulled the bottle from the cork of the next and drank one sink out of it, and threw the rest down the glass. I pulled the sink out of the next glass, and poured the cork from the bottle. Then I corked the sink with the glass, bottled the drink, and drank the pour. When I had everything emptied, I steadied the house with one hand, & counted the bottles, corks, glasses, and the sinks with the other, which were 29, and the house came by, so I counted them again. I finally had all the houses and bottles in one sink, which dranked. I'm not under the alcofluence of incohol as some thinkle peep, but the drunker I stand here, the longer I get. So you see, that's life!

All for now, dear old dad

Your "best" Son - My best Dad –

Love - Dad Mel xxxxx

September 17, 1944 Columbia SC

Dear dad -

Well, I received your letter telling me why you didn't write. And I understand. Marvin is sick for about the first time in his life, I guess. I remember when you had the "Yeller Janders" when we still owned the Cowen house and I was just a pup.

Glad to receive your letter as I was beginning to worry about you, really, Dad.

I taught some of them how to play cribbage and one kid from Massachusetts knew how, and now we play quite regular. Also dirty hearts.

We had 3 enlisted men and an officer killed last night when an engine conked out on the take-off. Whew. That's our greatest fear.

Sure hope you saw Packers & Brklyn play. I'm waiting on the edge of my seat to find out how we're going to be this year. If I'd been there, we'd sure as hell have went, hey?

Well, all for now. All my feeble tired brain can think of for now is what I mean.

Your "best" son,

Love to ya, Dad –

Mel xxxxx

September 21, 1944 Columbia SC

Dearest Dad -

Time to write again, I reckon. Nothing much has happened. I haven't been off the base even for 11 days. Somewhere around that, anyway.

Haven't heard from Bull Dunham, and I wrote right after he left the last time. Rat!

So Neuman & Price are gone again. I guess Dick was home once before, but Price wasn't.

Marvin must be in pretty sad shape if he's got an infected bladder. I don't envy him.

McTavey wrote again, and now he has 10 missions in. Said he was in on the invasion of southern France. Dropped plenty of stuff on em.

I was supposed to fly last nite, but it didn't appear on the bulletin board. Now the commander didn't believe me and another guy, so we're on alert for a week whether we fly or not. That means we go to the line and fly if we're scheduled or not every other nite and stay till the planes are off the ground until we're sure they don't need an engineer. It's only every other nite, so only four nites at the most. Not too bad. They had to cancel my flight as they only had one engineer and there was two of us missing. Well, they've got two extra ones on alert now for a while.

Tomorrow we have ditching. Go down to the water in trunks and practice bailing out of the body of a B-25. A wet job. I never had that before, so it'll be a new one to me.

Working you hard, hey? Well it's to be expected if you're short- handed. Always goes that way.

Love - Your "best" son Mel L. & K. xxxxx

September 24, 1944 Columbia SC

Dearest Dad -

Guess it's about time I wrote again. We've had a break in the schedule and I'm all rested up, so I feel like writing letters.

Elinor also wrote the other day & said Bud had died. But she said she didn't know for sure. It's really too bad. But it brings the war right home to your front step, don't it?

I'm just waiting for pay day so I can go into town and have a few brews. No money, no fun. I'm going to send you some when I get paid. Guess I owe you enuf.

Wanted to hear how the Bears & Packers made out, but the radio's on the blink. Hell! I'll read it in the paper tomorrow. What's the dope on Wisconsin this year? Not much I reckon. Purdue 27-18. Whoops! And the servicemen's paper "yank" picked her as one of the top teams along with N.D. Mich., and Ga Tech. Personally I'd pick Army, Navy, & Great Lakes, & N.D. The service teams are getting stronger and the college teams weaker. Colleges are using 17 year olds here & there. Let me know how A-F comes along. And who's all on the team. My old Alma Mater, etc.

Was in N.Y.C. at La Guardia Field yesterday for ½ hour. Kee-rist, is N.Y. ever big from the air. Guess I'll go there for Art School on the "G.I. bill of rites" after the war.

Guess I'd like to live in L.A. or N.Y.C. after the war. Don't know, tho.

I'd had to trace an oil line that broke on us while we were up in Virginia this A.M.

Thought for a while I'd borrow a dollar and go into town as I didn't have to fly tonite. Figured I'd go to a movie and have two beers. But changed my mind.

Maybe I'll go to Chicago tomorrow to pick up a re-modeled B-25, but don't know for sure. Only be there

15-20 minutes if we do. Will drop a card to you if I have time. Only takes 4 hours to go up there, and 4 back. I'm on alert, but may or may not go. Hope so. It'll seem good to get up there, even if it's only for ½ hour.

All for now, more later, Dad-old dear. Keep your chin up, & take it easy.

Love to ya-Dad.

Your "favorite" son Mel xxxxx

P.S. - X

October 2, 1944 Columbia SC

Dearest Dad -

Well, the eagle shit to the tune of 110.00. Here's 50.00 on account. More next pay-day.

Went to Tallahassee Florida Friday nite. Slept in the nose all the way down, and flew all the way back. We've no co-pilot, so I have to be able to bring her home in case. Sat low and couldn't see out, so used the instruments and was all over the sky.

Maybe I'll get the furlough when this training is all over. Sure as hell hope so. I'm going to send 50.00 a month home, so if I do get home, I'll have a working capital. And if I don't, you'll have the money anyway. Sensible.

This paper really got cheaper as soon as I got off the letterheads.

All these new guys who were so enthusiastic about flying the first few times are starting to pray to Allah to rain like a bastard when their turns come up just like us old veterans are.

Well, I won my quart of Scotch off old Cavanaugh, hey? Spose I'll hear from him one of these days. Rave on McDuff!

Tonite I'm going to Fredericksburg Virginia. Was up there once before and she's a long haul. Especially at nite.

Saturday we were supposed to fly over Fort Jackson on their maneuvers and spray them with tear gas in wing tanks. They handed us a ship with no rudder so it was no go. Bet that didn't make the infantry boys mad at all. Me either, because it's a messy job, and she will leak up through the bomb bays and give us a little dose of it also.

Saw the Army's new A-26 the other day. Boy, what a crate, take it from me.

Wow! Wis 7 - N.W. - 6. Who the hell'da thunk it? What's the dope on old Wis? What cha think? Saw Georgia Pre-flite take S.C. 21-14. Saw Marlin Harder on the bench next to "Ducky" Pond. He was in uniform, but couldn't play. Ronnie Cahill, ex Holy Cross and Chgo Cards Pro took his place, and he was plenty hot.

All for now. Shower and shave, and prepare for the nite flite.

Love - Dad Your son - Mel xxxxx

October 21, 1944 (I guess) Columbia SC

Dear dad -

Well, here's your long lost bastard of a son. Figured, seeing as how I only flew 1 hour & 35 min today and have a long lost rest today, I'd catch up on a little mail.

They've been flying the nuts off me. Four-five hours a day. Including Sundays.

Had some pictures taken at the fair (State Fair) 2 nites ago, and I hadn't taken a drink at the time. Maybe that's what's wrong. I don't know.

I'm so damned sick of flying right now I can't even carry on an intelligent conversation about a B-25.

When I get out of that damn plane at nite, I don't feel like anything. Just a beer or the bed so I can pop at it at 7 the next morn. I'll try to do better from now on. As I've said before, no doubt. Liar that I am.

Guess I owe about 12 people letters now. Can't worry about that. You people come first.

We're almost ready to go out. Got about six missions left. Guess the 12th of next month.

Listened to Great L.-O.S. play, 6-6 when we landed and I shut it off. I'll bet Wis got stomped today. Haven't heard yet. Little Clemson beat S.C. Thursday. Tickled the hell out of me. Ohio really stomped G.L. under 26-6. Wow!

We were out in the woods for 10 days dis-assembling a wreck. I volunteered for it and we lived in tents. Never again. Hell, I'm just a civilian on detached service, myself.

I'll send $50.00 home again the first. Wheww!! If you want to spend it, go ahead, old bean. Take a week and go to Madison or somewhere. It'll do you good. Life's too short to work your pratt off.

Wisconsin didn't do bad against N.D. at all 28-13. Whew!!

Don't guess I'll get home again before I go over. Might, though. Look for anything in this crazy army.

Guess I'll go to the show, & bed early, and get my rest back. Can't think of any more to write about right now, anyway. More in a day or two.

Love - Your "best" son, Mel xxxxx

To the best old dad I've got. Yep!

October 25, 1944 Columbia SC

Dear Dad

Well, I've got one of the damndest colds I've ever had and they've grounded me for a few days. I've had the same one for three weeks, but it's just lately that it really bothered me.

I guess they're short of engineers, and if we finish sooner than expected, we'll just fly extra for other crews. So I'm in no hurry to finish. Guess that means no furlough. Oh well.

Saturday I'm going to go to Battle Creek, Michigan for an overnite flite. I'll be pretty close to you, but it'll be as if I was on the moon.

Yesterday morning we flew in a 24 ship formation and the P-40's were making jumps at us. Got in a lot of upper turret time. Got to keep in practice, or you lose the touch.

I won a fruitcake on a board the other nite. Everyone helped eat it. Guess that was our Xmas in the U.S.A.

All I do in the plane in the air is read books. Guess I've read every one for miles around.

Sure wish I had a nice nite club to go to tonite. Feel like a good time, but there's none in this dump. Got one of those wild streaks again.

Enuf for now of my troubles. I guess I can't make up my mind in the army, anyway. Nuff said.

Love, Mel xxxxx

October 27, 1944 Columbia SC

Dear Dad -

Guess it's about time I wrote again. Haven't written for 3-4 days.

Well, I have a bad cold & I'm grounded. There's only one man in my crew that isn't grounded, & that's the tail gunner. If you have a cold and continue flying, you'll get germs in your ear, and that leads to infection. You see, your ears open to a little tube to the throat and by them, you equalize pressure on your ear drums as you go up or down. So the germs get in there. They call it Aero-otiters. Very common, & not serious. They use a heat lamp to dry up the infection. My ears are ok but I have to get rid of the cold first.

It's too bad, but I'm going to miss that trip to Battle Creek, Mich tomorrow. Haven't got a pilot anyway. As I said before, he's grounded too. We'll be in the air again in 3-4 days.

We've got a few missions to do before we're ready yet. Guess we'll be alerted the 12th of next month, and then we'll leave for P.O.E. at Savannah soon after that.

They've got a major back from overseas here now. Now we've got take off at a certain time, and arrive over the target at a certain time, etc. All of it's timing, same as overseas. Then we have bombing and cannon runs and fighters jumping at us. We use a camera gun, & the pilot does evasive action. Zig-zags to throw the fighter's aim off. Good stuff, I guess.

What's the matter with Johnny Christofferson? Nerves, it sounds like. I feel sorry for him. Nerves are no fun. I've seen some good cases right here on guys who've come back from over there.

Well, Pop, all I can think of for now. Be good, and take care of yourself. And I will too, naturally.

Love from your son, Dad. Mel xxxxx

I'm going to trade my watch in again cause all I have is trouble with it.

ORDERS TO WHERE?

November 3, 1944 Columbia SC

Dear Pop -

Your boy is going to finally fight the war. After nearly two years, it's here. I'm alerted for the twelfth like I said. Yep. It's Hunter Field and Savannah,Ga for me. P.O.E.

Here's a money order for 50.00 again. Use it any way you damn well please, boy. I don't care. It's yours anyway.

Well, guess that's no furlough for me. Some of the guys finished up and got four day furloughs. I could just get home on that, and that's all. It'd do me no good.

Saw actual movies of a B-25-H stop a Nip destroyer cold with the 75 m.m. cannon. She's really a killer. Yep.

All for now-Pop, ole bean.

Love your son, Mel xxxxx

November 27, 1944 Hunter Field GA

Dear Dad -

Finally I've gotten around to writing you again. Here I am in Savannah at P.O.E. Hunter Field. Guess I'm finally going to fight their war for them.

Here's a picture of me taken in New Orleans the 10th of last mo. I went down there on another crew when their engineer didn't want to go. Spent three days there. Not enuf time to get home and back, so I went thru to Wash. D.C. & went thru the Wash monument and the Smithsonian Institute. Then decided I'd go to Philly and see that Fish girl. Went and stayed at her house and saw Matlock's folks. Stayed over there all one aft. And Fish & I came out of there pretty well lit up. Then we went to see some of his other friends. More drinks & a good dinner, and we all got tanked up. But good. Suppose you've been wondering what in hell I was doing in Philly.

I was real busy in Columbia. They took almost all our clothes away up there. All new issue here I guess. Here we get the new British parachute complete with a jungle kit containing a machete, fishing tackle, compass, D ration, mosquito net, cartridges for a .45 colt, which they also issue us with a shoulder holster, and other stuff.

If we go out of here by air, they take & give you only one blanket. By boat, two. If you go to the South

Pacific you only have khakis, and Europe you take O.D.'s Smart deduction.

Most of our type crews (H) are going to China or Italy. Guess it'll be China. Ok by me.

Don't know how long I'll be here, but you can write here if you wish. I'll get it. Anywhere from 3 days to 3 weeks, they say. Then either to New York or San Fran for boat or plane.

Here you can still buy cigs unlimited, and cig lighters which are no good for me, and sell for 14.00 here, and 22.00 on the civy market. In fact the U.S. pays 19.00 for them and sells them at a 5.00 loss to us. They spend more money on an aircrew man than any other soldier.

I got here last nite and thought I'd write today while we haven't anything to do for a change.

I'll go in town tonite at 5 o'clock. See what they've got to offer. Not much I hear.

I'll write again as soon as I know more about stuff. I'll know pretty soon where I'm going, I guess. And I'll sure let ya know, Pop.

Be good and I'll write again soon as I'm not so rushed for time now, as I was, Pop.

You be good now, and I will be also.

Love to the best Dad of all,

Your "best" son - Mel xxxxx

November 29, 1944 Hunter Field GA

Dear Dad -

Wrote Gram today for the first time in weeks. Should write her more regularly also as she's the only one of the tribe I hear from. Except a letter from Perry a while ago, and one from Vic, which came as a complete surprise.

Well, I know nothing more except that our order number is the same as the guys who have been going to China.

All I've been doing is reading, playing ping pong, sleeping, eating, and writing a few. Very monotonous.

Got a letter from Bob Dunham. He's in England. Said the girls weren't as good as here. Leave it to him to think of the girls first.

They got a joint called "The Casino" about halfway to town. We go there and drink beer til midnite. It's just a dump, but it's something to do. Reminds me of Joe's nite club in Mauston.

All for now, Pop.

Love to my old Dad - Your son-Mel xxxxx

Dec. 1, 1944

Dearest Dad - Hunter Field GA

Got a letter from Gram today. Might as well enclose it so you can see how things stack up. Better than trying to tell you. Don't know why I didn't do it before.

Next month will make 2 years at my present occupation. Longest I ever held a job. Yep. The bastards just won't fire me no matter what I do.

I saw "30 seconds over Tokyo" last nite. It shows some real pictures of the old B-25-C model. See it if you want an idea of what the ship I'm in is almost like. We have the H with the turret in front now, and the cannon. They really made a fool of the engineer in it, tho. But I guess its alright. What the hell. This is a democratic army. Like shit it is!

I'm a real sharpie. I'm wearing my first pair of G.I. shoes in months around here. It's been raining and now it's muddy as all hell. On top of that, we haven't had our final showdown inspection and we can't turn in any laundry or dry cleaning until we do. No crease in my pants, or anything. What a deal this is.

Well, this is all I can think of for now, dear old Dad.

Love from your son, Pop!

Mel xxxxx Lotsa hugs & kisses, too.

December 6, 1944 Hunter Field GA

Well, here I am going to write what may be my last letter to you in the U.S.A. I filled out my A.P.O. cards today and tomorrow I'll turn them in, and the day after I leave, they'll stamp them, and mail them.

I got you an Xmas present yesterday and mailed it as you'll know by the time you get this letter.

We were issued all our new stuff this aft. We're going by air out of the country. And we're going to the S. Pacific where you wanted me to go.

We didn't get any parachute or Mae West. The airplane will have them.

Here's some of the stuff we were issued:

> summer flying suit
> goggles with 8 sets of lens
> .45 Colt -2 clips - shoulder holster
> winter flite jacket & pants
> oxygen mask - built in microphone
> winter helmet - built in headset
> summer helmet - built in headset
> 2 new pr. shoes
> 6 pr. sox
> 5 pr. under shirts & shorts
> 3 kaki shirts and pants

    mosquito nets - insect medicine
    soaps & towels
    dagger & scabbard

We'll go by train to San Francisco I guess. I'll drop a card if I can on the way.

We turned in all our O.D. except one pants and shirt for the train. Haven't even got a blouse now.

Got a card from the Dunhams. Nice of them. Clifford's a good guy. Will send them an A.P.O. card also.

I made out a voluntary allotment to you for $50.00 a month today. Told you I would once. They said you'd get the first payment about the 3rd to eighth of January. Ok?

We might end up in Burma, China, or Leyte Island. Who knows, and who cares? I don't.

All I can think of, Pop!

Love from your "best" son, Love - Mel xxxxx

Be good old boy. I'll see you in a little while.

December 7, 1944 Hunter Field GA

Dear Pop -

Got another letter from Gram. Here it is.

Also I'm sending some old letters, and an inhaler, finger nail file, etc. Also my Kee Bird I bought in New Orleans, La.

We'll fly to Hamilton Field at San Francisco Sat. nite as the latest dope goes. Then we'll gas up, and continue on out.

All for now Pop, ole boy, ole boy!

Your best son, Mel xxxxx

December 9, 1944 Hunter Field GA

Dear dad -

Received a second letter from you today and was damn glad to hear from you.

We're shipping out of here at 8:00 P.M. Only 1 hr and 10 min to go. We'll go by Pullman to Hamilton Field, San Francisco. Then by air to the S. Pacific.

Well, I'll write on the way if I get the chance.

Love - Your "best" son Mel xxxxx

GANGPLANK TO EUROPE

On November 10, 1944, at 10:17 a.m., Clarence and the 106th Lion Division boarded the USS Wakefield; destination, England. The Wakefield was formerly the luxury ocean liner, SS Manhattan, and was commissioned by the Navy in 1941 for troop transport.

Clarence tells of their departure. *"Before we left Camp Atterbury, all of our equipment had to be taken apart, coated with cosmoline and loaded on the train. That's how we got from Camp Atterbury to Miles Standish and then to Boston.*

"We had all of our trucks and guns on the Wakefield and there were about 7,000 of us, I think. I don't remember if we all went on one boat or if they split us up. I think they did and the infantry went to a different port in England."

Clarence was correct in his thinking. The 422nd, 423rd and 424th were on different ships and they left approximately two weeks before the service battalions.

"We walked up a gang plank to board the ship and realized space was minimal. It was going to be a long seven days crossing the ocean. We were only a few miles out when we had to change our direction quite often in case of enemy submarines.

"I was supposed to be down three floors below the water line. The bunks were 6 feet long and stacked real high. I remember the high waves. They were terrible. I stood on the deck and my overalls were so stiff I could have broken them off like cardboard.

"After unloading, we convoyed down to Guilford Surrey, if I remember right. We stayed there while we put everything back together."

153

The 106th stayed in Nissen huts from the 17th to the 29th of November at which time they were assigned to VIII Corps, First Army, 12th Army Group.

Clarence continues, *"On the 1st of December, we boarded L.S.T.'s and crossed the English Channel. We went up the Seine River and anchored somewhere near Rouen France. We saw several sunken vessels and blown bridges along the way. The river was like the Mississippi. You would come out in the ocean and then go up the river just like by New Orleans. La Havre was a port on the river and it was all blown apart.*

"December 6th was my 21st birthday and the next day, I went to Rosee, Belgium, and then back to France again.

"I wish I would have kept a complete diary of those days. I suppose I always thought I'd remember it all, but I don't. I guess in a way, that's a blessing."

DECEMBER 15 1944

O n the morning of December 10th, the 106th Division officially entered combat. The battalion moved from a bivouac in the woods approximately a mile
and a half northeast of St. Vith Belgium marching through heavy snow along dan-
gerously slippery roads. Reaching their destination, they waited for the 12th Field
Artillery, 2nd Infantry Division to vacate the area that they were now to occupy.

The 106th was referred to as being 'green' and 'untried.' As the veterans
of the 2nd Division were leaving, their remark to the new guys was that
they were getting a *good deal*. All was quiet on the Ghost Front.

This area of the Schnee Eifel, the snow-covered mountains between
Belgium and Germany, was considered a quiet sector where they could
train for combat. During the day of December 15th, the division noticed
more activity than normal. Several reports of this nature were conveyed to
superiors; however, they were ignored.

Along with the warnings, Major General Alan Jones, commander of
the 106th, was taking the location of his men very seriously. The entire
division, including his son, Lieutenant Alan Jones Jr. with the 423rd, was
positioned at least six miles out into the Siegfried Line. Because of the terrain, both hills and fields, they were extremely susceptible to attack from
each side as well as above. In fact, he protested that it was possible that the
entire salient could be surrounded and cut off.

His orders, however, left him no choice. The men were to remain
where they were. By midnight, the reports told again of much rumbling
and movement along the front. Once again, these reports fell on deaf ears.
While the military leaders slept soundly in their warm beds, more than
250,000 Germans with their arsenal of artillery and tanks quietly readied
themselves for the pre-dawn attack.

DECEMBER 15 2012

I sit here tonight by the fire, warm and cozy in my home. I awoke this morning and without even glancing at the calendar, I was well aware that exactly sixty-eight years have passed since the eve of the *Ardennes Offensive*. December and the holidays have taken on a completely new meaning for me now.

If this is the direction my thoughts take these days, imagine what runs through Clarence's mind. He had just mentioned a few days ago that it was *'on this date'* he had boarded an L.S.T. and was crossing the English Channel. Then he was quiet again. I know now that the whole month will be like this for him. He will fade in and out in his reverie and at this point, he will tell me what he is thinking or he won't. I also now realize that the memories are very painful and difficult to relive and talking about it is not how he wants to spend his last days.

This afternoon, my husband and I attended a Christmas party. There was an older gentleman there in a wheel chair wearing a WWII Veterans hat. Before we left the gathering, I of course took a moment to walk over and thank him for his service. He seemed surprised by the gesture, which I have come to expect. I learned where he was stationed and he graciously shared a few of his experiences about his time in the service.

He is now eighty-five years old; quite young, I thought, to be of this war. I wondered how that could be, but then he said he was overseas already at the age of seventeen. He never thought he would live to see eighteen or that the war would leave him disabled.

When I told him what Clarence has always said about being guinea pigs, he agreed. "We all were!" was his exact forceful comment.

157

He also had a personal story to tell, one that I don't think he shares easily. Before I left him, I asked if he, too, dreams about the war. He sighed heavily, and yet spoke softly. "All the time," he said. "All the time." As I watch and listen closely, I know that I have witnessed the same haunting look time and again these last few years as I questioned Clarence.

I am completely lost in thoughts of war as I watch the clock slowly tick its way toward morning. There is no way I can imagine what sleeping in a cold foxhole would be like, nor will I even try. Thankfully, I wasn't there.

Instead, as morning arrives, my purpose at this, the exact hour, and yet so many years later, is to simply bow my head in prayer, honoring those that were.

POOR INTELLIGENCE

In Clarence's words, *"We arrived at the front line and took positions at Laudesfeld, Germany. The 592nd had 12 guns, 12 half-tracks and then the trucks. We supplied everything. You're talking a shipload of stuff to move and the roads over there were like a narrow driveway. You had traffic going both ways on a 12 to 14 foot wide road. The half-track was about 20 feet long and then the barrel of the gun another 12 ½ feet. That's how big they were. In order to turn a corner, you had to bulldoze buildings."*

Every conversation I had with Clarence, he never failed to comment on the commanding officers 'error in judgment.' They were so certain the Germans would not come through this quiet sector of the Ardennes during the winter, and yet they had done so once before.

Clarence laughs, *"Does it say anywhere that we didn't have any shells? They sent us to the front lines with nothing to shoot with. I went to Namur Belgium the night before for ammunition. My job was ammunition sergeant. We had what you called the Red Ball Express. It was a bunch of colored guys that drove semi and they'd haul all of the ammunition from all of the ports like Le Havre. We got back with our first load and never even got them off the trucks. I got back at two o'clock that morning and the Germans attacked at 5:30 a.m. The trees around us were snapping like toothpicks. It was 14 degrees when they started shooting. We didn't even have overshoes. All we had was leather shoes and they were soggy wet."*

In the early light of dawn, with screaming meemies piercing the fog and the rumble of tanks rolling toward them, the 'lucky' young doughboys of the 106th were about to receive their rites of passage into battle.

159

The troops were spread thin, had no combat experience and were lacking essentials needed to survive. What they did have was guts and determination. And a will to live.

Clarence continues, *"You talk about poor intelligence? How could Hitler amass all of that on the other side and not know about it? They probably had to start in September in order to bring all the troops, the guns, the tanks, all the shells and the gas. They had miles of gas stacked along the roads. You mean to tell me they couldn't see? It was reported two or three times to the big shots and ignored. I think we were guinea pigs.*

"Hey, take 8,000 men between here (home) and Wisconsin Dells (27 miles) and expect them to defend against five armies. And the tanks, well, if they'd have had some shells and then the poor infantry, they didn't have enough bullets. No food. In three days they ran out of everything. Ah, man. Oh, well. Well, it just goes to show you, none of those in command were that brilliant.

"The 592nd, we were mobile, where the Infantry, the poor Infantry, the 422nd and the 423rd, they were right in it solid. We were in it solid, too, the only thing is, we were shifted around a lot. You moved at night and you stopped. You might spend a day somewhere camouflaged, and then move again, always at night. Our job was to supply the shells for the guns and the radar fuses. Wherever the guns were, we had to go.

"If they wanted us in Brussels one night, we'd have to go to Brussels. If they wanted us there for a week, we'd stay there a week before moving again. Then we might have to go back to Bastogne or St. Vith. St. Vith was where our headquarters were.

"We were always about two miles behind the Infantry because of our big guns. We couldn't shoot low other than point blank. Our shells had to go up and then down, that's why we were back farther. The guns carried about twelve rounds and it took about five hours to set it up, but only about six minutes to shoot. When you put the bullet in the barrel, you left room for powder behind it before it was closed and then you stuck a shell in there. When you pulled the rope, that ignited the black powder and that shot the flame out of the barrel just about the length of the house. We had to camouflage the flame

at night otherwise the Germans would see it. And I also had to know if they were shooting any kind of gas...all of the mustard gases.

"On the end of the shell, they had a radar fuse you could set so the shell would explode whenever an object got in front of that little hole. That was also part of my job, setting the fuses on the shells and getting them ready. We used to set it to tree top so when a shell would come down like that, the treetop would explode and trim all the trees down. The shrapnel would break the branches right off. The Germans were dug in the ground and the hunks of iron, the shrapnel, would go down and kill them. And the same thing with the trucks. We'd use the shrapnel.

"The Germans on the Siegfried Line, they had little slots where the machine gun barrels were. We used to put a shell right in there. Right in there where they were looking out. That's how accurate they were. But that was all done by elevation, the speed and everything. And the powder that we got from Badger Ordnance in Baraboo used to come in all different sized bags; different heights and different thicknesses. It depended on the distance you were shooting what you would use. If you had to shoot 8 miles, you put them all in. If you wanted to shoot 3 miles, you stuffed a small one in.

"We were the only 155 howitzer in the division and we supplied the artillery for all over. The 590th, they were lighter, their shells weren't as big around as ours. Neither were their bullets. The 589th was ahead of us. Their shells were smaller and they got them from us. They really took a beating. As a matter of fact, they lost everything.

"We had no communication. The Germans cut the lines. You didn't know where the different outfits were or anything. You have no idea what it's like. You have no idea. And the sad part of it was, because Eisenhower and Montgomery, the two biggest smart asses, kept saying they wouldn't come through there, we were sent up there without a goddamn thing.

"You know it's weird how you can figure out how you can kill people," a forlorn looking Clarence continues. "That's like that knife I have. That was the last resort. In other words, if the guy jumped you, you just held it in front of you and it would go in his gut. Where the Infantry, they had it on the end of the gun barrel, but see we had to have our hands free with the shells and

161

stuff. But that was the last resort and then we also carried a little carbine and a 45 pistol. Yeah, I could tell you a lot.

"A lot of young guys. And the other sad part about it, we were together as a team in South Carolina, but when we got to Indianapolis, they took a lot of the guys that had been with us from the start and sent them out to other outfits and gave us a bunch of guys that hadn't been trained with us. And in the Army, you don't question it. You do as you're told and that's it.

"And as far as commanders, Colonel Weber was pretty smart. They criticized him because when he heard of the breakthrough, he knew how many shells we had. Truckloads, because of just coming back from Namur. We were loaded with shells and he wasn't about to let the Germans get twelve guns and 700-800 rounds of ammunition. So he pulled us back right away from where we were at the time. And of course he was criticized for that but I mean, he was smart. We didn't lose a damn thing.

"I still think we were there as bait. A brand new unit that hadn't seen any combat and to cover 27 miles when normally a division of that size only covers five."

After the first initial barrage that lasted a little over an hour, one German soldier hollered from a few feet away that the Americans should take a breather because they would be back. The enemy was within shouting distance, and as daylight broke, you could see dead bodies covering the expanse between the combatants.

With the telephone wires knocked out, mass confusion prevailed. All that could be heard over any American airwave was German band music. Out on the salient, the 422nd and 423rd knew the artillery was heavy, but were unaware of how desperate their situation was. By December 17th, those two regiments were cut off. When Major General Alan Jones, commander of the 106th thought help had arrived, it was in the form of one man who had come ahead having no idea how serious things were or when his men would be arriving.

To make matters worse, Jones was of the impression that supplies were being dropped to his men. Little did he know, that when he ordered the supply drop to continue on the 18th, that as of yet, nothing had reached the troops.

Through all of this, you wonder how any of the men were surviving. This is where the guts and determination came in.

However, by 3:30 on the afternoon of December 19th, just a mere three days after the assault, Colonel Descheneaux, commander of the 422nd Infantry, made what was to some the unpopular decision to surrender. They were being slaughtered and he hoped to save as many lives as he could. The order was given to break up any guns and pistols and he went back to his trench, buried his face in his hands and wept.

Later, when he saw the grenadiers relieving his men of their cigarettes, he insisted that each man be allowed to keep one pack. The nodded agreement came from a German lieutenant.

Just fifteen minutes later, at 3:45 p.m., the same decision was reached a mile or so away. Colonel Cavender's men of the 423rd would also surrender. They, like the 422nd, were out of food, water and ammunition. Even though it made no sense to try to fight, giving up was a bitter pill to swallow. The customary order was given to destroy all weapons. Before long, the Germans were marching up the hill rounding up the men of the 423rd.

AFTER ACTION REPORT: DECEMBER 1944: It is presumed that the 422nd Infantry Regiment, 589th FA Bn., 590th FA Bn. and the 106th Reconnaissance Troop were eventually overpowered by the German forces east of St. Vith and the bulk of the personnel captured about 19 or 20 December. The strength of the German attack in the division sector and the forces available to the division at the time prevented their being relieved. Attempts to supply the units by air failed because of the weather, although, as learned later, two drops were made but not within their reach. It is known that they were still in the fight early 19 December. It is also known that prisoners were taken by the Germans. However, the final chapter in the defense of the Schnee Eifel penetration of the Siegfried Line held by these units is not now known. The estimated losses sustained during this period were 8490, including 415 killed in action, 1254 wounded in action and 6821 missing in action.

Despite all odds, by January, the 106th Division secured their place in history for their part in helping to slow the German advance to a crawl. Hitler had diverted precious troops from the Eastern front in order to launch this all-out effort in the Ardennes. It was a gamble and one that was lost. Due to a lack of fuel, unexpected stiff resistance and the clearing weather, a crushing defeat was imminent.

As the tide was beginning to turn in Europe, the war in the Pacific raged on. Melvin arrived in New Guinea in January and the legacy of his missions was about to begin.

AULD LANG SYNE

The small town that our family hails from still boasts about the same population now as it did back then. That number is, 'not much.' It was still quite astonishing that my grandfather received a letter from one of the other 'boys' from home who had run into Melvin overseas.

Sunday January 28, 1945. 'Somewhere in New Guinea'

Dear Manley,

I know you will be surprised to hear from me, and especially from down under where the army has me now. Well, I met your son here last Wednesday and thought I would tell you how everything is with him. He sure looked good, and when he came up in front of me, I almost fell over. We were in a group listening to a major tell us about our new home when he spotted me and he came over to make sure it was me.

We had a good talk, and he came over again in the afternoon and we hashed over Adams and all the home folk. It was really good to see him; it had been sometime since I had seen him, too. I think the last time was January 1943 when he and I ushered in the New Year together. He left here Thursday morning for up north, and I think you can guess where by the news.

Lt. William E Keefe

Melvin had a ten cent Fred Harvey Serviceman's Map that he used to keep track of where he was stationed at all times. He had written dates and locations all around the outside edges. On the 24th of January when they met, they were both in Nadzab, BEI, New Guinea. The 'up north' he was referring to was Tacloban.

I have been able to piece together even more of Melvin's life from all of the letters he and his father received from different servicemen from home. My grandfather was apparently quite a popular old chap and was considered just one of the guys. Knowing him, he would have liked that.

PERSONAL MISSION LOGS

I have freely admitted to being completely ignorant about some of the boxes' contents. Heck, I think I have freely admitted to being completely ignorant about WWII, have I not? Thankfully, that is no longer the case. The letters were one thing, but as my knowledge grew, so too did the discoveries.

As time went on, I became much more adept at recognizing what I consider some very priceless items. I made it a habit of perusing the contents every so often, but it was over a year later that I found three small meticulously folded pieces of paper that I did not remember seeing before. I wonder now how I could have missed Melvin's personal mission logs.

Following is the first of those pages showing his method of keeping track of those missions and his points that he needed to go home.

The first missions that he flew were when the 345th were based at Tacloban, then San Marcelino and on other sheets, Clark Field and Nadzab. Most of what he wrote made sense to me.

The far left number is his mission count, then the number of the plane, the name of the pilot, the duration of the mission, the date it took place and where they bombed and strafed. As noted, some of the planes were eventually lost. I had no idea as to what the asterisks and check marks were for and could only guess what the numbers on the far right side might have meant.

I contacted Lawrence J. Hickey, the author of 'Warpath Across the Pacific'. He agreed to see me and help with any questions I had regarding my father's time with the Bomb Group.

Melvin's personal log

On April 4, 2011, I arrived at Mr. Hickey's home knowing I was taking up much of his valuable time. We spent about two hours sitting at his dining room table talking about the 345th and Melvin's logs. He felt that the numbers on the far right with a plus sign were no doubt extra points toward going home as he was well aware that these were some very difficult missions. He then told me that because of this, Melvin had good reason to wonder if he would 'go the distance' while he was at San Marcelino.

If my book sparks any interest in the 345th Bomb Group, please read "Warpath Across the Pacific." It is a masterpiece.

Following is a map showing the area of operations for the 345th. Based on his letters, his mission logs and this map, it is interesting to follow their push north toward Japan. I also noticed the scale of his map. No wonder it took hours and hours to fly these missions.

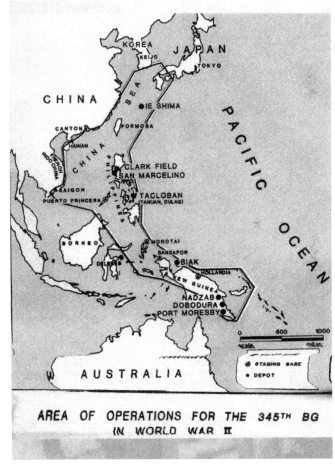

Map of the 345th's area of operations

WHITE-BELLIED BASTARDS

January 27, 1945 A.P.O. 72

Dear Dad,

Well, this is the first chance I've had to write you at all. I've received a few letters from you so far. Some of them V-mail.

Of course I arrived here by plane from New Guinea.

I was in three places in New Guinea, but not for long. We came over by boat and the trip was uneventful. We only got two meals a day, and the food was piss poor, but I'm used to it, I guess. I can't tell you dates or places, of course.

I saw Guadalcanal and it looked pretty peaceful. It should by now.

There's so much I could tell you if I was allowed, but it'll keep till I get home.

Squadron 500 is called the "Rough Raiders" and the group (345th) is called the "Apache Raiders". Tokyo Rose, I hear, calls us the "white bellied bastards" because of how our planes are marked, so I guess the Japs know we're in the war alright.

I'm in the Philippine Islands now. There was a lot of fighting here a while ago judging by the looks of things.

Malaria isn't rampant here, and we use mosquito nets and take atabrine tablets here anyway.

You ought to see the foliage here, Dad. Thick and green.

Morale is excellent here. No one bitches too much. We have six men to a tent and we use cots and have our own blankets, etc.

This is my first letter. We're not allowed to keep a diary so I'm keeping all facts in my head. All for now. More later.

Love, Your son – Mel

DECLASSIFIED INTELLIGENCE REPORT-FEBRUARY 1945 The 345th entered its second month of crowded Tacloban life with almost everything under control. Torrential downpours brought to light hidden athletic abilities as rank and file leapt like gazelles from dry spot to dry spot. Pacific rains, as Bob Hope put it, was short for "man the boats boys, the island's sinking."

CONFIDENTIAL MISSION REPORT-1 FEBRUARY 1945 Six A/P's of the 500th Squadron completed a single minimum altitude bombing-strafing pass across the float plane base at the primary target, Puerto Princesa, Palawan in the morning of 1 February. A total of 72-100 pound parademos and 5,200 rounds of .50 calibre ammunition were thrown at installations, damaging buildings, an unserviceable Tony and a serviceable truck. Results: Bombing was excellent with all bombs but two falling on land in the target area.

Bombs are seen falling near the American Prisoner of War Camp on buildings along beach – believed to be too far away to damage POW installations. Smoke covers the target.

DECLASSIFIED INTELLIGENCE REPORT-1 FEBRUARY 1945
The 1st's strike against Puerto Princesa was the only Philippine Island mission that did not go to Luzon. Twenty-three planes hit water-front facilities, scoring two direct hits on one large building and stringing bombs through radio installations adjacent to an apparently abandoned American POW camp.

February 2, 1945

Dear Dad,

I wrote you a while ago but didn't send it airmail so you'll probably get this one first. Don't know, though.

I got a couple of your V-mail letters when I was down in New Guinea.

I've put a couple of missions in already. One to Cabacaben on Bataan Peninsula to bomb and strafe. It's close to Corregidor. We avoided the island on the way back. Then one to Puerto Princesa on Palawan. We bombed & strafed there also.

I can't think of much to say now. I've got to stay up all night so thought I'd write you again. Not too much happens here that I can tell you. Most of it'll keep till I get home anyway.

Guess I'll make S/Sgt in a couple of months. Hope so. Notice the address on the envelope. It's my new one.

We're reputed to be the most hated flight group in the South Pacific. 'Tokyo Rose' mentions us quite often in her little broadcasts. She has pet names for us that aren't complimentary. She plays records trying to make the guys homesick, and asks us little things like "did you enjoy eating your bully beef and hardtack this morning?" and then proceeds to describe a ten course dinner to us. There's all different kinds of theories on her identity. Some say she's a middle aged white woman who went to a school in Ohio. Others that she's a Hawaiian born Jap well educated in Hawaii, etc. She's similar to Lord Haw-Haw the Reich used on the British. They probably copied her from him. The Japs are not original, just damn good copy-cats. They use some planes of German design. The ME-109 is one.

I've seen lots of wrecked Jap planes. They're all over wherever you go.

I've gathered some Jap money also, but will keep it. Would like to get a hold of a Jap pistol. They're rare and cost plenty, I hear.

Well, all for now old Dad. Be good, & don't worry. Things aren't too bad here at all.

Love & hugs, Your son – Mel

The name Puerto Princesa piqued my curiosity early on even before I read the mission reports about the abandoned POW camp. I decided to find out more about this place that sounded like a cruise ship's port of call. Who was I kidding?

ABOUT PALAWAN

The American POW camp was definitely abandoned by the time the 345th had their orders to bomb and strafe on the island of Palawan. What was it like then and now? Well, I never did find out about now. In my mind, I can't get past 'then.'

In Puerto Princesa on the island of Palawan, 346 American POW's were detained there to build an airfield for their captors. They were beaten daily and if they attempted escape, they were executed.

Their diet, what there was of it, consisted of wormy rice and a cup of 'soup' made from camote vines boiled in water. If they could not work, their rations were cut by 30 percent. They had fallen into the hands of the *kempeitai* (kem-pay-tie), the Japanese military police and intelligence unit. The *kempeitai* was feared by all because of their brutality.

Just before an American Liberator bombed the island, approximately half of the prisoners had been returned to Manila leaving the other half to finish the arduous task of completing the airfield. Even though the bombings raised the hopes of the prisoners, it angered their captors. So much so, that their rations were cut and the beatings intensified.

Because the Allied aircraft was now always present, the prisoners were allowed to build three shelters for themselves. On the morning of December 14, 1944, there was an early morning bombing raid and the prisoners hid in the shelters. At two o'clock that same afternoon, under close guard, they were ordered inside once again under the pretense of another raid.

The *kempeitai* then doused the shelters with gasoline and lit them on fire. Of course, the men attempted to escape and were executed on the spot. If any man made it to the cliffs and jumped hiding in the rocks, they were

177

found and also executed. Of the thirty or forty men who escaped, only a few managed to get away.

One Marine, Glen McDole, who had survived an appendectomy with no anesthesia, was one of these men who lived to write his story. I must admit, I read two chapters of his book and for the first time since I was little, a nightmare woke me in a cold sweat.

Even though this story is not Melvin's or Clarence's, it is a harsh reality of war, one that adds to the horrors of what was endured by so many brave young men.

In 1952, the camp was abandoned for good. The remains of 123 prisoners were brought back to the states and buried in a mass grave at Jefferson Barracks National Cemetery near St Louis, Missouri.

I was at Jefferson Barracks in September 2012 to honor members of the 345th who are buried there. After a B-25 fly over, I bowed my head once more, along with the others, in honor and in prayer for so many that gave their all for our freedom.

SAN MARCELINO

CONFIDENTIAL MISSION REPORT– 5 FEBRUARY 1945 Four B-25J's of the 500th Squadron made a low level barge and shipping sweep along the entire East coast of Luzon from Legaspi in the Southeast to Port San Vicente in the Northeast during the morning and afternoon hours of 5 February. Objective: the strike was designed to intercept any Japs trying to evade our troops in Central Luzon by barge or other shipping from the East coast of Luzon. No land targets were to be hit; only barges or larger shipping was considered a target.

February 9, 1945 A.P.O. 73

Dear Dad,

Well, guess I've been a little long in answering your letters, and letting you know I'm alright.

I've got four missions in now. We get 1 ½ points for 5 combat hours. I've got a fraction over 8 points. Twenty seven hours - 45 minutes time. We need 100 points to be eligible for return to the USA.

We went up the Luzon coast looking for Jap shipping. Found some oil barges and a small freighter.

Don't worry. I'm alright. Be good Dad.

Love, Your son Mel

After promising to write more, well, he didn't. I don't think he had time. After they moved to San Marcelino in the middle of the month, his mission count was on the rise. On the 18th of February, he even flew two missions, one in the morning and one in the afternoon.

CONFIDENTIAL MISSION REPORT- 18 FEBRUARY 1945: On the 15th, now under the 309th Bomb Wing, we entered the Bataan phase, running five consecutive ground supports, mostly along the road from Bagac to Pilar. The most impressive of these missions occurred on the 18th, when we sent a total of 61 Rogers over the target, enabling the Infantry to follow..."behind rolling barrage of fire and bombs laid down...in the largest and longest close support mission in this sector... troops advanced then without opposition to within five miles of the west coast of Bataan."

CONFIDENTIAL MISSION REPORT – 18 FEBRUARY 1945 This strike, like the morning mission, was in direct support of U.S. troops advancing west along the Bagac-Pilar road in Central Bataan. Zombie instructed our crews just prior to the attack, defining those areas to be hit. Considerable numbers of enemy troops were supposedly hidden by the heavy tree cover in these designated areas.

The 500th strike photo on the next page is now in my private collection. Every now and again, I can excitedly tell you that more discoveries are being made. This was one of about forty strike photos we just found along with an old scrapbook of Melvin's containing over 250 photos from his time in service. Many seem to be when he was in Columbia, South Carolina, before going overseas. Thankfully he wrote names and dates on the back of a good share of them, but many may always keep me wondering.

I believe Mr. Hickey was correct in his thinking that they received extra points for more difficult missions. Melvin had marked an 8+ in the right margin of his personal log for February 23rd. After reading the extensive report, I have to agree. It details the destruction that they caused to Jap shipping, but the price was high. This strike was flown by the 500th alone and was part of a program designed to destroy enemy lines of communication from the Netherlands East Indies and Singapore areas to the Japanese homeland.

February 18 mission (Bagac) providing ground support

CONFIDENTIAL MISSION REPORT-23 FEBRUARY 1945 In a smashing attack on shipping along the East Indo-China coast, nine B25-J's of this squadron sank two 2300-ton tankers and a lugger, seriously damaged a destroyer escort, and damaged to a lesser degree another DE and a launch on the morning of 23 February. Nine planes of the 500th came in on the target in elements of two, line astern at 50/150 ft. Lt

Bagley, although hit at the beginning of the run, thoroughly strafed a DE effectively silencing it's guns. Lt. Bagley's right engine was ablaze at the time he was covering his leader. Lt. Bagley's A/P crashed and exploded within 50 yards of the DE narrowly clearing the top of the vessel. A/P 191 was lost to A/A and all crew members are carried as killed in action. Lt Bagley will be recommended for the Silver Star. Lt. Bagley's crew will be recommended for Distinguished Flying Crosses.

February 26, 1945 A.P.O. 73

Dear Dad,

Another day. Another dollar. So much for that.

We've done quite a bit of flying right along. Been to (this small section of his letter is cut out due to censors.) Also some places here in the Islands.

All the boys from Columbia are here. Six of us live in the same tent.

Two of us are high in missions, both having ten. My tail gunner and I. One of these days I'll make S/Sgt. (I hope.)

I'm sending you a 100 peso, 2-10's, 5, 1, 50 centans, 10, 5, and 1. That's all the variety I have. And just about all there is.

The Japs paid the Filipinos in this currency. It was so inflated they say it took a lot to buy a bag of rice in the end.

Our water is purified with halazone and I've gotten so I can't even taste it by now. Right here mosquitoes are at a minimum.

Love you, Dad,

Your son – Mel

CONFIDENTIAL MISSION REPORT - 10 MARCH 1945 Successful shipping strike at Tourane Bay on the East Indo-China coast, six of our A/P's sank a large tanker of 7,000 tons and damaged smaller vessels. Opposition: A/A: Light, meager, accurate from vessels; one A/P holed. Four Tojo's caught up with our formation as it left the target through the mouth of the Bay. Two came in high from 6 o'clock closing to 800 yards before breaking away when our gunners opened fire.

March 14, 1945 A.P.O 73

Dear Dad,

I've been receiving letters from you regular. That's good, because I sat for five weeks once waiting for all my mail to catch up to me.

So you still have your cribbage games. Well, the chips keep you in beer anyway. You're probably like me, you'll do almost anything for amusement.

I know the cigarette situation is really poor there. But we get all we need given to us for use. Camels,

Luckies, Chesterfields, and some Raleighs. Once in a while we buy some for 50 cents (1 peso) a carton.

Do you ever read of this outfit in the papers? It's supposed to be fairly well known.

I've got thirteen missions in, and more coming.

There really isn't much to write about here. The exciting part, the flying, you can't say much about.

Take it easy Dad, old pal, as I'm doing. And be good too. Here's a hundred bucks for your birthday. Let me know you got it.

Love - Your son - Mel

In between the last letter and this one, Melvin flew eight more missions. Some were to the Indo-China coast, one to Nha Trang, the Yamashita Line, and a ground support mission over the Infanta area on the East Coast of Central Luzon.

On March 28th, the 500th led the group of A/P's on a primary attack designed to cut enemy lines of communication and the secondary target was largely of harassing value. Two of the nine planes taking off did not reach the target. One had engine trouble about an hour out and was escorted back by another A/P. The escort plane was flown by Lt. Goodban with Melvin aboard. All planes were low on gas when returning, two of them landing at Palawan and five landing at Mindoro to re-fuel and then proceeded on to San Marcelino. His log reads that he received 'time only' for that day because they turned back with A/P 356.

GONE BUT FAR FROM FORGOTTEN

March 29, 1945 (345th Bomb Group)

Dear Dad,

I haven't written for so long I have a guilty conscience again, or yet. I've been hearing from you regular though.

I've been plenty busy and have twenty one missions in now.

I've flown over Manila. It's really a pretty laid out place. The war was really there, though.

I made S/Sgt. the 27th of this month. Two days ago.

Things aren't tough here. Sick of dehydrated food and I'd give $25 to hear a toilet flush. And a white girl would be out of this world.

I sent you 100.00 for your birthday. Fifty years old. Go to Milwaukee or Madison for a few days and enjoy yourself. I remembered Mom's on St. Patrick's Day. How could I forget? Gone but far from forgotten is

185

the sad story there. God Bless her, and if there is a heaven, she's up in it looking down on all us fools over here in the Islands.

Happy Birthday Pop. You're the best old Dad anyone could ever hope for.

Love,

From your "favorite" son, Mel

In June of 1945, the March 29th raid was a featured story in the then popular 'Yank' magazine. It is quite a detailed mission report which I found very interesting.

CONFIDENTIAL MISSION REPORT- 29 MARCH 1945 Attack: The 501st and the 498th Squadrons attacked the convoy first and were followed by the 500th and the 499th Squadrons. Our eight B-25J's initiated their attack on a Northerly heading, flying for the most part in two-plane elements at minimum altitude. Fog and rain squalls partially hid the convoy and our pilots had to fly on instruments frequently during the attack. Opposition: The greater part of the intense A/A came from the main pier area but many light positions were firing along the river banks east of Hoi How, in the town itself and from a flak tower located just east of the hospital in town. Losses: A/P 888, piloted by Lt. Simpson, was hit during the run over Hoi How. Other crews reported that fire broke out in the stricken plane's open bomb bay and around the top turret. The crew of A/P 888, are carried as missing in action. Comments: Weather prevented an accurate count of the vessels in the convoy, but an estimated eight units is probably a conservative figure.

DECLASSIFIED INTELLIGENCE REPORT for this mission reads in part as follows: 16 Rogers of the 499th and 500th Squadrons contacted convoy at approximately 1500N-10930E and attacked 1130/I to 1210/I. 1 Sugar two stack, est, 10000 tons was sunk. 2 ELB were sunk, (one following violent explosion), 1 DE sunk, 1 DE probably sunk, 1 DD probably sunk (direct hit and explosion) 1 SBL damaged, 53x500 lb. demos were dropped and 40,000 x 50 cal. ammo expended. All calibers A/A moderate to intense, holed 5 A/P. Low clouds and rain squalls in convoy area obscured vessels and hampered attacks as well as preventing identification and damage assessments, accurate.

Melvin was in Lt. Goodban's plane when the 500th flew this next mission.

CONFIDENTIAL MISSION REPORT- 23 April 1945: In the early afternoon of 23 April five of our planes after completing an unsuccessful shipping search from Yulin Bay, Hainan to Sifa Point on the east coast of Hainan, dropped 20 x 500 pound bombs on small towns and installations on Hainan's east coast approximately 33 miles northeast of Yulin Harbor. Results: Lt. Goodban strafed 25 slit trenches staggered along the coast in the bombed area.

April 24, 1945 A.P.O. 73 Bomb Group (M)

Dear Dad,

Haven't written for some time.

I flew another mission the other day so that makes 23. Lots of anti-aircraft, but no hits. They're lousy shots. This squadron really has a good record. Wish I could tell you about it. Oh well sometime I will.

Love, Mel

May 6, 1945 A.P.O. 74

Dear Dad,

I've got no excuse for not writing sooner, Dad. Just plain lazy, I guess. I'll try to make up for it by a few more letters.

I haven't been doing too much flying lately. That's ok by me as I'm not too eager one way or the other. I've still got 23 missions in.

I was on a rest leave in Manila. Ran into a guy I was with the first time in Columbia. It was in the Red Cross.

That article you read in the paper was ours. We're the Apache Group all right.

I sure was crazy over airplanes once upon a time, but when this war's over, those days are gone forever.

Your letters are coming through like a bat out of hell now.

The films I sent to Australia aren't back yet. However, we had some others taken and I had 'em developed in Manila, so I'll send three of them along. More later. We split the others up for now. I'm standing by our tent in one, holding a .50 cal. machine gun and the other's an old wrecked Jap plane.

Tent mates, Melvin holding rifle

I've got a Jap rifle I picked up. Don't know if I can send it home, but I'll try. It's cheaply made, but all their stuff is. It's long, and a .25 calibre. I don't see how those shorties handle it.

Yes, I'll probably be home in less than fifty missions.

All for now Dad, old boy

Love, Your "best" son, Mel

VE DAY

After Hitler committed suicide on April 30th, 1945, the Germans began to surrender in record numbers. On May 7th, the war in Europe was officially over and May 8th was declared VE Day or Victory in Europe day.

With the surrender came a tremendous rush to set up POW camps. It has been written that by May 18th, there were over 900,000 prisoners which the Americans and Allies now had the monumental task of housing and feeding.

Clarence recalls the prisoners having their own kitchen and mess hall and they, too, had their own. He said it was necessary to get in line by five o'clock in the morning in order to get lunch. In fact, he said, you really never got out of line if you wanted to eat. That's how many men there were.

Clarence and the 106th Division were assigned to guard prisoners in Heilbronn, Germany. A portion of his group had one house they were living in and while there, he was sent to the university to get his certificate in sports and physical education. His job was not only to provide recreation for the prisoners to keep them occupied, but also to his comrades when not on guard duty.

Another of Clarence's memories is when he arrived in La Havre, the mailbags were stacked as high as the trees. Right after the war ended, he wrote home asking that his baseball shoes be mailed to him. He arrived home in December before they even got there and they had to be sent back.

Each day they attempted to discharge as many prisoners as possible to try to keep the numbers down. Clarence said once he and five other enlisted men, along with two officers, took a trainload of POW's from Heilbronn to

Marseille, France, to set them free. Hitler had 'recruited' them to fight the war for him and they were now allowed to go home.

Clarence is very proud of this time and tells quite often how he could have taught any sport when he came home from the war. He even mentioned he would have liked to have been a gym teacher. With his love of sports and great leadership qualities, he could have easily followed his dream. I know he would have excelled in that role. Even after the war, he played in Highland Park on the city team. We are not certain if the uniform he still has was from that team or from high school. Either way, what I do know, is that it was wool, *heavy* wool, and had to be very hot and itchy to wear. But another fact is? It was made in the U.S.A. So not only was he happy finding it recently after all this time, it was not made in China, a real bane to his existence.

He is still hoping to find his actual uniform from Heilbronn that has 592nd on it. It would indeed be another great keepsake.

In later years, in the resort that he and Lucille owned, a wonderful German couple stayed in cabin #1. The man loved to fish. After the two of them chatted for a while, they realized that he was one of the prisoners that Clarence had guarded during the war. What a coincidence. As the conversation was ending, they shook hands as if they, too, had been comrades. As they parted, they agreed that they were just doing what they were told. It was war after all.

Malesky and Clarence in Heilbronn

INTENSE AND ACCURATE FIRE

CONFIDENTIAL MISSION REPORT - 30 May 1945 Performed by 500th Bombardment Squadron (M), 30 May 1945. Four of our A/P's in a late morning minimum altitude attack hit ammo revetments on the south edge of Tainan (Einansho) airfield, Western Formosa and a sugar and alcohol mill with warehouses and personnel facilities, 7,000 feet east of the revetment area. Opposition and cost: Intense and accurate fire was received from the six gun medium position in the sugar mill area...A 20mm burst that killed the radio operator on A/P 588 probably came from this area. The radio gunner, S/Sgt William G. Hudak, was killed by the explosion and resulting shock.

In a later letter, once the war is over, Melvin tells of the day Hudak was killed. Eventually, of the forty who went across the states together on their way overseas, there were only twenty-six left.

June 5, 1945 A.P.O.74 (still 500 Bomb Squad. 345 Bomb Grp)

Dear Dad-

I'm still here in the Philippines and nothing has changed except I've put in another mission. Twenty four now. Coming along damn good. Should have ¾ of my requirements by now. I heard from Bill Keeffe too. Said they had seventy holes once when they got back. Pretty lucky. I know a few to match that. Wait'll I get home - boy.

Well, pard - all for now.

Take it easy, Love – Mel

June 10, 1945 (Somewhere on Luzon)

Dad,

Today the weather is rainy and a fine day to curl up with a tomcat in your lap in front of the fire. Or a blonde.

Three days ago we got twelve bottles of beer - and I still have three. Times sure change. I remember when that wouldn't have lasted at all. A guy sure learns to conserve what he has.

The food hasn't been too good here. You can live on it if you're not too fussy. And I sure as hell am not anymore. I can eat anything you set in front of me now. Remember how I used to be at home in the good old days when Mom was still alive?

I suppose you had her grave decorated as usual this year. I flew that day over Formosa and I'll never forget it as long as I live. Some day when I come home you remind me and I'll tell you about it.

It's hard to write as there is no news. But I guess the main thing is that I write, and you know I'm alright.

We had shots the other day and my arm was sore. Gotta have a couple more next week.

To the best Dad From his "best" son

Love, Mel

The day before this next letter was written, A/P 149 crashed and exploded in a rice paddy killing S/Sgt Roy Hartmann, another of the men in the picture with the Air Apache sign in his upcoming letter of August 8th. The cause of the crash was not definite although the pilot, flight leader Lt. Geyer, was flying near the drome at Okasaki at forty feet and was in the process of dropping his parafrags when they crashed, according to the mission log.

Strike photo showing parafrags over Okasaki

June 16, 1945 (Somewhere on Luzon)

Dearest Dad-

Well, here I am again. Nothing to write about, so I'll take the three letters I've had from you since I last wrote and go from them.

The first thing is Tokyo Rose. She was a white woman and was in Manila & was captured when Manila fell. And this guy that told you he sent her records was a goddamn liar, and you can tell him I said so. Nobody even knew where she was, let alone who she was. That burns me up when some of these jokers come out with that crap.

That brings me to the negative business. When I sent that letter it had a negative for every picture. Someone screwed up the details. So you wouldn't have noticed those B-25's in the formation. If you were over here and saw those dots, it'd be time to turn on the gun sight and charge your machine guns and start tracking them. And I'm not kidding either.

Well, I guess I'll have four battle stars, two air medals, and a Unit Citation or two when I get done. Maybe more.

This outfit has two Unit Citations already and more coming I guess. They got two for Rabaul, and I wasn't in the outfit then, so can't & won't wear them. But this other one or two I helped win so I'll wear them.

Well, all for now. Still twenty four missions -

Love to you Dad, Mel

June 25, 1945 H.Q. Base Serv Sqdn. 360 Air Serv Grp

Dear Dad

Yesterday I arrived back in New Guinea for two months of detached service from my outfit.

I'm 2500 miles from Luzon now. Made the trip by B-25 in 2 days, stopping at night.

A radio man, pilot, and I came down to be instructors for the new guys from the states.

We get combat credit for our time, but the students don't. We get 3 points for 10 hours, and I had 79 points, so need 21 more or 70 hours.

My pilot and navigator quit. Nerves. And my radio man was killed. We lost three out of eight in my tent. Didn't tell you before as it'd worry you - but now it doesn't make any difference. Out of forty of us, twenty-six are still alive. That's the forty of us that went by train across the states.

We had some rough targets and I saw ships go down but I only was holed once. Plain luck! Look in June 22 "Yank" magazine. I was on that raid.

Well, Dad all I can think of for now - be good, & take it easy as I am.

Love, Mel

July 15, 1945 360 Serv Grp A.P.O. 74

Guess it's about time I wrote you again. I've been moving around a little again, of course.

I flew one training mission to Wewak down in New Guinea. Now the outfit has moved up here where the 345th is at. I'm staying over here in my squadron till they get our area built up.

I've got 80 points, and need 20 more. Then the good old U.S.A. Oh, boy! Now I have 26 missions in. Not much flying compared to February & March, hey?

Nadzab was 7 degrees below the Equator so I could tell where I was. Here I can't, but it's old A.P.O. 74 again - but a new outfit now.

I've got some good strike (mission) pictures now. More coming when I finish. Picked up 34 from my group (345th) alone. About 75 in all.

I was supposed to make T/Sgt. but it hasn't come through yet. Who gives a damn anyway? I don't – for damn sure.

All for now Pop,

Love from your "best" son, Mel

Melvin's strike photo of Wewak

August 3, 1945 (Luzon)

Dad,

Well, another month is here, and still the same old story. Last month I didn't do a damn thing towards getting me home. Still have my 26 missions. I haven't even been in an airplane for three weeks.

Right at the present it's raining to beat hell. One of these babies that comes up all at once with the fury of a young tornado.

You said some of those missions were probably harder than I let on & you're right. And all I've got to show for them is an Air Medal. They don't hand them out easy over here. I'll tell you all about them some day.

The war's really in high gear, but it'll be higher yet. Wait'll the boys in Europe are all over here. Maybe the end's in sight; I don't know.

Guess I'll bring this to a halt now, Dad. Rain's let up now pretty good. The FEAF-CRTC means Far Eastern Air Forces - Combat Replacement Training Center

Love to the "best" Dad,

Your "best" son, Mel

Melvin, taken in Ie Shima

Each time I read that letter, I still wonder at his comment about the end being in sight. He could not have known how right he was. At the time, I am certain it was wishful thinking.

It was between that letter and the next that another of his tent-mates lost his life. Marvin Peddicord was killed on a mission over Korea when the plane he was in exploded before it hit the water.

August 8, 1945 Luzon P.I.(360th A.P.O. 74)

Dear Dad -

Received another letter from you, and I'm really making an honest effort to write at least twice a week.

I sent you a picture of me sitting in a chair in the last letter and I'm sending you four pictures in this one. They were taken March 4 at A.P.O. 73, just at the time I was flying steady.

I had a nice short haircut at the time, hey? We're certainly a good looking bunch of cutthroats, aren't we?

Well, nothing has happened here, except that I was up to one of the islands in the Ryukyu chain. My group is up there, but I can't tell you which one. I stayed there two nites & got back yesterday.

I guess you must really have a quite a few pictures of me & the guys in my tent by now. I send them as

I take them. Gadbois sent these to the states when I sent those other four to you to enlarge. They're all the same roll of film.

L to R; Marvin Peddicord, Robert Gadbois, Roy Hartmann, (seated in front) Melvin, Charles Kistner

I still haven't flown, & don't know when I will start. Maybe I shouldn't have taken this deal. But then again, who knows?

Well, Dad, ole boy, take it easy. I am.

Love – Mel

Manila newspaper announcing the end of the war

August 14, 1945

Dear Dad

The other nite we heard the Japs had offered surrender on their own terms. And I guess the President will speak this A.M. at 11 o'clock. That's 10 P.M. last nite by Wash D.C. time. Maybe then we'll learn if it's all over, or if we're to keep on fighting.

I hope by the time this letter reaches you, it'll be all over but the occupation. I have no desire to be shot at again.

You seem to think that when I came home once for 30 days, I'd be coming back over again. That's not the case.

Have you ever found anyone who knew where this A.P.O. is located?

I got your clipping on the B-25 that hit the Empire State Bldg. Had already seen two or three though. Audrey Frazier sent one also. They make quite a roar when they go off, don't they? I've seen a few crash, & they're all like that.

Still have only 26 missions. Would have more if I was still in the 345th Group.

Well, all for now. Be good, Pop, & I will too. Maybe I'll be seeing you one of these days. Who knows?

Love - Your son Mel

CAMP LUCKY STRIKE

Back then, it seemed that almost everyone smoked cigarettes. In some of Melvin's letters, he even comments on the fact that they could get the popular brand names overseas and all that they could want, unlike back home.

It was one of the few pleasures that the servicemen had. Remember, even as Colonel Descheneaux's men were surrendering, it was asked that they were allowed to keep a pack a piece. Little comfort would be my thought on that.

After France was liberated, several camps were established outside the port city of Le Havre. These camps served as depots for newly arriving replacement GIs and more importantly, they were used later for those that were leaving to go home. For security reasons, these camps were named after popular cigarettes of the time including Lucky Strike. That happened to be the brand that Clarence always smoked and where he and some of the 592nd awaited their departure. Clarence arrived there around July 20th.

Another man who also served with Clarence in the 592nd FAB wrote that when he got on a ship from Le Havre after the victory in Europe, it was headed to the Pacific, much to his dismay. He was at sea for five days when the ship changed course for New York. Japan had surrendered and he was elated to be going home instead.

345TH ESCORTS
BETTY BOMBERS

**August 24, 1945 Hdqs. Sqdn. 360th Serv Grp
A.P.O. 74**

Dear Dad -

Well, for the past few days I've been sitting here at Biak Island in New Guinea. I figured I'd be back up in the Philippines so I put off writing.

I guess the war is all over now, but I don't know when I'll be coming home. I still ended up with my 26 missions. Don't know if I'll have to finish on other flights, or if my CRTC time will be good, or not. I've not been up to the group for two weeks. One thing, I'm still alive, & that's a lot more than I can say for some of my old friends. And believe me, I didn't know if I was going the distance a few times. Maybe you've been worried that something didn't happen to me in the last days of the war. Well, old Dad, don't worry, as I'm perfectly all right.

I've got a lot of interesting pictures of things over here. Don't know if they'll all pass censor. Time'll tell. You've got a lot of them already.

Love, Your Son Mel

September 4, 1945 500 Bomb Sqdn. 345 Bomb Grp A.P.O. 245

Dear Dad -

Well, here I am back at A.P.O. 74, but in a couple of days I'll be back at my outfit on A.P.O. 245, so you write there.

When I get there, I'll know if I'm coming home & when. Also I'll know how many stars I've got - 4, 5, or 6. I think I'll have 75 points for discharge, but don't know.

If the 345th did escort the Japs to Manila like you said, I wouldn't know, as I haven't been up there since the 9th of the month.

Yes, I've seen the Silver Dollar Bar in Manila but it's all wrecked and rebuilt. Not much to it now.

Did I tell you I had two front teeth knocked out in Manila in April when we ran off the runway? Washed the ship out, & drove Jap narrow gauge railway track through the bomb bay. I'll have them bridged in when I hit Frisco.

Censorship has been lifted so I can tell you I was with the Group at Tacloban, San Marcelino, & Clark Field. Right now I'm at Clark. The outfit is at Ie Shima where Ernie Pyle was killed.

Now that you won't worry any more, I'll tell you that 5 out of 8 in my tent were killed, including my radio man

& tail gunner. There's Gadbois, Lenhart, & I okay. You didn't know the boys, so it's okay, but when you'd go out & someone wouldn't come back, it didn't set so good.

Well, so much for that. I'll tell you when I see you.

Love, Your son Mel

September 11, 1945 Ie Shima

Dearest Dad,

Well, yesterday I came up to the Group in a B-24 of the 43rd Group.

I hear that in less than a week I'll be in Korea. We'll be on the outskirts of the capitol. It's 900,000 & untouched by the war.

A crew was up there last week, & the Japs came out smiling & bowing with ice cold beer & sake. Also gassed the ship up & serviced it.

Yes, our group escorted the Japs from Kyushu & to Ie Shima. I've got pictures of the whole mess. Everyone got a set of them. On the front of the folder is a picture of Ie Shima with V-J on it. It's 11 ½" x 8".

On the 2nd page it has three pics of the 345th and the two Betty Bombers with the crosses on them. Then a pic of the first one landing & then taxi-ing to the C-54.

On the 3rd page they're getting out, then walking over to the C-54. Standing there & bowing, next pics they're receiving instructions from Gen. Thomas, and then onto the C-54 & on to Manila.

On the fourth and last page, there's pictures of some of our missions. Kyushu, Formosa, Nha Trang, Hollandia Swatow-Amoy, Mako, Rabaul, shipping on Indo China coast, Daqua, Gorontals & others.

I had my picture taken with 3 Japs in a jeep. Pretty good. So far, I've got 37 pts. for time, 8 for overseas, four battle stars, & an Air Medal. 70 points. There's two more stars coming, & I'll be eligible to come home. I ended up with 80 ½ combat points, & 26 missions.

Melvin's picture of him and three Japs

On May 30, we went to Kagi Airdrome in Formosa (a couple of my experiences.) Remember, I told you I'd never forget May 30th? Well, we fanned out & came in over the trees at 290 M.P.H. I didn't see any flak, just some revetments and radar huts. But we came off the target & a ship just ahead had one tail shot off. Then the ship next to us had the tail turret shot out. Then they said over the radio that my radio man was killed instantly by a direct hit of a 40mm. I felt like crying.

When we landed, we had three holes also. One would have hit me if a stringer hadn't stopped it.

In March we hit Nha Trang in Indo China and I saw a 500th ship go down in flames just ahead of me as he was strafing a destroyer. They were guys that had come overseas with me. We made a run on the same destroyer, but didn't get hit, luckily.

We hit a convoy once & sank seven ships in five minutes. I strafed Japs jumping off a sinking DE (destroyer escort) and saw about twenty fall dead. So now I know I've killed, but it doesn't bother me. They'd have killed us if they could've. That's the way it goes in war, I guess.

Well, all for now Pop.

Love, Mel

The VJ booklet he talked about along with four pictures of Betty Bombers were among all of the pictures found not long ago.

213

I said in the beginning how the passage of youth was evident, even on paper. He grew up fast, the hard way, as did many young men his age.

Even though that was one of his more compelling letters, this next letter that I will share with you I think is more so. He actually wrote this letter two years ago on the 2nd anniversary of his mother's death. Maybe he wasn't as immature as I thought at first. I think too, that in my mind, because of never knowing him, I sometimes forget that all I have read was written when he was in his very early twenties and not in his nineties which he would have been now. That's a long time to be without him no matter how you look at it.

I only think of him as real young or real old. I haven't taken the time yet to think about all of the in between. Soon, I suppose. I will call them 'patient decades' and when I have more time, I will sit alone one day and contemplate the in between that I haven't given much thought to. This is the letter about his mother.

Sept. 30, '43 Amarillo Army Air Field, Amarillo Texas

Dear dad –

Well, I 'spose you're thinking the same thing I am today.

Just two years ago today we had a great time didn't we? I believe I felt just as sad the day they buried her as the day she died.

I can't help but think of how great a woman she was. How she always did her best for you and I in spite of all the odds that were against her. How she helped me make up that 3rd grade and all when I was so badly banged up.

How she saved her money so diligently even down at the Legion Convention just to no avail. And the money she had in the bank book all ready to put away. And all to no avail.

How she made me save my money when I worked for old Nye.

As she looks down on us now, I can't help but think she can't help but be proud of you for the way you've borne up these past two years and kept your nose on the grindstone...for yours was the greatest loss – not mine.

And, by the same virtues, she can't help but be a little bit disappointed in me. I had a good job at Briggs & Stratton & quit. Got another at Merrimac, and never saved a cent, in spite of $65.00 a week.

Then I got in the Cadets, and only had 8 weeks to go for a commission, and threw it away. I've screwed up every damn thing I ever did, I guess.

She had a touch of genius in her makeup, dad. She could have been a great artist, and a lot of other things.

I remember how tickled she was when I'd bring her home something. And it was so very seldom I did that, I feel like the original Lucrezia Borgia.

And how we used to have a few cups of coffee and rolls after I'd come home from school. And she'd say,

"Mel, you be sure and eat a good meal now when Dad comes home." And I'd say I would and invariably let her down.

Well, all I can say now is, here's to the greatest woman of my knowledge and God rest her soul, and God bless her as she deserves it if anyone does.

Love, Your son, Mel xxxxx

Edna Marie Newkirk Pollock sounded like a wonderful woman. Her and my mother would have been great friends as they seem to have been two of a kind. I am so sorry I never knew her either.

LUCKY TO BE ALIVE

September 20, 1945 Okinawa 500th BS 345 B. Co.

Dear Dad,

Well, I guess this is the last letter you'll get from me overseas. I'm on my way home.

They took all the guys with 60 or more discharge points I had 70 - or 10 months overseas I had nine - or 85 combat pts - I had 80 ½. So I made it.

Three of us in our tent left yesterday, leaving two. We're in the 312th Bomb Grp now. They're going home & we're with them, waiting for the boat now.

I used to wonder if I'd ever make it when we were at San Marcelino. Now I know.

I don't know if I'll get a discharge or not. I'll write you when I hit Frisco. Then you'll know I'm in the States.

I got Gadbois' pistol yesterday. So I don't have to worry about shelling out $27.00 for one. Still haven't got a B-4 bag. Maybe can get one here.

Guess I've taken my last ride in a B-25 when we came over here yesterday P.M. Good. I was getting sort of afraid of them towards the end. Seen too many burn up. I'm lucky to be alive, and I know it.

Don't write me anymore. I'd be a long time getting them now. This is all I'll write also.

My T/Sgt rating is in, but it'll take a long time to catch up. Also I haven't got my Air Medal. I fell 16 hours short for a second one. Also I got credit finally for shooting down a Jap plane, but no Air Medal. Also got a destroyer once but the tail gunner was excited, and the camera wasn't turned on. Only pictures can give you confirmation. So, I could've had four Air Medals instead of one. But who cares?

Well, all for now. Love Your son Mel

October 7, 1945

Dear Dad

Wrote you sometime back & said it'd be my last letter from an A.P.O. but we missed the boat. All with less than 80 pts, that is. If my 5th & 6th battle stars would come in I'd have exactly 80. Got 70 now. All I've got to do is get on the boat & get to the States, & I'll get a discharge.

So I guess my army career is finally almost at an end. Can't believe it - you know?

Don't write to me anymore. Our Group won't forward much more mail. Got a lot of mail running around the Pacific from New Guinea on up, but I'll never get it.

I haven't heard from certain ones at home now. They worry over trivialities when I've been over here where the chips were thrown in and you were playing for the biggest stakes of all - your life. Oh, well. I should write a book. But it's the truth, no matter how dramatic it sounds on paper.

That's what's wrong with 90% of the guys when they come back. No adjustment to the simple things. Don't give a damn. In some ways the army has ruined me - and other ways helped me. But you and I will be closer than ever.

I've learned to play chess. Quite a game. We play quite often here. Nothing to do. But tomorrow I'm going to see Naha. I'll eat dinner with the navy & come back in the P.M.

No air medal for that Jap plane, but I don't need the 5 points anyway. So what.

We've got so many men here you can't even get seconds on coffee in the mess hall.

We're on the end of Yantan Air Strip. Planes taking off & landing are directly overhead all day.

We'll have a good time when I come home. We'll go to Chicago, Milwaukee and Madison and go and see

Mom's grave. I want to put some flowers on it for everything she did for me. I wish she was there in our old house waiting when I come. Would she ever be tickled, right?

God, she's been gone four years. And I've been gone three, you might say. I know you've been lonely, but it's almost over now.

Guess I've written a book.

Love to the best old dad from your "best" son Mel xxx

October 12, 1945 Okinawa

Dear Dad

No doubt you're worried now as this typhoon we had here has made the papers back home.

Well, four guys in the 380th Bomb Group were killed when a building blew over. All in all, five soldiers were killed, hundreds injured, & 1,500 sailors missing off ships in the harbor. By the way, I'm in the 380th Group now, but didn't know the guys who were killed.

The winds reached 104 M.P.H. but I didn't think it was too bad. One tent I was in split, & a guy broke his back. I beat the hell out like a scared rabbit. Well, at any rate I'm ok and there's nothing to worry about. This was my main object in writing. Nothing else in this great part of the world is new, except we might fly to Manila & sweat out going home from there.

Okinawa has been condemned as an army post till they can get permanent installations instead of tents.

You can write me here. If I go to Manila, my mail will be forwarded. And it looks like I'll be overseas a while yet. It's a question of transportation. Too little for too much. Guess I'll be a full three year man yet. Have till Jan 17th to go. Sure seems a long time ago since I reported to the Franklin St. Armory in Chicago. I've gone thousands of miles by air, train, & sea since. Guess it's done me some good. I don't know. I don't guess you can get a job as a machine gunner after this is all over unless you join a mob.

I laugh at their offers to re-join for a year. Some guys will, but not me. They haven't got enuf money in D.C. to keep me over.

Love, Your son, Mel

October 15, 1945 Okinawa

Dear Dad

Well, I'm writing again, & again I'll tell you not to write me as I'll not go to Manila. I've got 80 discharge points now & I'll be home on the next boat. I was processed this morning & my next base will be Camp

McCoy & I'll get a discharge there. Sort of seems too good to be true, but it is.

They've got a plan now to send gunners home that have been over at least six months or have 200 hours, or 50 combat points.

I had 70 pts & had the battle star for Raboul & a cluster to the Air Medal added. Came out on orders dated Sept 6, but I just found out about it yesterday, so now I've got two Air Medals, & five battle stars, with two more stars coming, plus a Presidential Unit Citation or two.

Don't know if I got the cluster for hours, sinking a destroyer, or the Jap plane. Guess it was the plane though. I'll have to get a look at the orders to be able to tell, & I haven't seen them as yet.

I've also got some pictures of the typhoon here and some snaps of girls they paint on the planes noses. I've got a snap of Gen. Buckner's grave. Too bad I didn't have a camera the day I went & saw Ernie Pyle's grave.

There's nothing new here. I'm all set for the return voyage now.

My army hours run over a thousand. Been at it 2 ½ years, you know. Combat hours over 190, and 28 missions.

Well, all for now. Maybe I'll write Gram & tell her I'll be seeing her one of these days in the near future.

This will no doubt be my last letter. If nothing else develops. Maybe you'll see me in four or five weeks.

So Ohio State stomped "ole Wis" 14 -0. To be expected.

Love your son Mel

October 20, 1945 Okinawa

Dear Dad

How do you like the stationary? Hope you get a charge out of it.

Here's four pictures for you. Two of them are pretty good. In fact all four are. Two are self-explanatory & the other two aren't.

One's of me in Manila on the 9th of Sept, the day before I left by B-24 for Ie Shima to rejoin my Group. Taken in the walled city where the fighting was heaviest. Notice the wall. That's a Jap flag I had, but some bastard stole it lately.

Melvin in Manila

The other is taken on a mission to the Inland Sea of Japan on Aug 12th when I was still in C.R.T.C. The ship indicated by the arrow, a Captain Davis & a flight leader for one squadron, was separated & never seen again over the target. Still don't know what happened, but a Catalina saw B-25 wreckage in the target area later, so guess that was it.

Saw a bad one two days ago. C-47 came over our area wobbling. We all watched it stall out & crash. Blew up & burned. We hopped a jeep over, and saw five burning bodies in the wreck. The first pilot was thrown clear but died yesterday. I've seen a lot of them, but this one was pathetic. Some jerks were taking pictures of the bodies close up. Why, I don't know. Really makes you leary of these iron birds.

I'll drop you a line the day I leave here for sure, & maybe before that. I got a rat turd on my Air Medal for that Jap plane (cluster), & now have 80 points. Will make a boat pretty quick.

My orders read McCoy now. They're all sealed & packed. My overseas tour is all over but the shouting. In fact, my whole army career.

All I can think of for now.

Love Your son Mel

November 1, 1945 Okinawa

Dear Dad

Well, I haven't written for a few days now, and although nothing much new has happened here, I'll write again.

I guess a lot of my mail has been lost, or something, but it don't matter.

Well, today is Nov 1st although it's Oct 31st there, so it makes 10 months I've been over on this side. Seems like a long time. Lots of water under the bridge & lots of things have happened. Not many of them good.

I've got my flying time for October & November. Rode in a B-32 for six hours last month, & 5 ½ hrs this month, the records show. So that's a few dollars more.

They're processing the 38 year olds today. All of the 83 points & over men have gone since yesterday. Now they'll get down to the 80 pointers. I heard we'll be loading today, or a day or two.

Today the 60 pointers are eligible for discharge, so I feel like an old veteran with my 80. Also I heard my sixth star came in. The China campaign. If it did, it'll be on teletype pretty soon from Fifth Bomber Command in Japan.

Okinawa is beyond a doubt the worst hole I've ever been in, bar none. Some of the boys thrive on it I guess, as they re-enlist. Not me. I can't get out of the army fast enuf.

When I get back to the States I've got to write Kistner's folks in Bismarck, MO. My tail gunner. His wife was daughter of an Ohio Congressman, & he lived in Dayton, but I won't write her. He was 27 years old, & a real guy. But he's dead now, & that's that. Also Hudak, my radio man. He was from Cleveland, & 20. He was just a kid all over, but a good one. I'll have to write his folks also. Boy, I often ask myself how come I made the grade when so many others didn't. Guess I'll always ask myself that. And never get an answer. Maybe if I hadn't went to C.R.T.C. I'd have gotten it too. I'll never know of course.

About all I can think of for now. Haven't heard from anyone for a while so no news to pass on to you.

Love, Your son Mel

Melvin had finally written his last letter from overseas. He spent Thanksgiving on the USS Crockett having turkey and all of the trimmings. The little menu they were given, which includes cigars and cigarettes, has the date November 27, 1945, written on the back. He had gone the distance after all. At least so far.

BUTTON YOUR BUTTONS

"*I should have stayed in. I would have been 39 years old and have a pension for the rest of my life. Of course it wasn't much of a pension then, though. And, I could have been killed in Korea. A lot of my buddies got killed in Korea.*" Clarence is telling me this one day after we found notes he made in his service record book.

There is one notation in his notes that he made after December 16 that I find haunting; Continuing their attack for nearly a month. My Div. trapped; lost 8,663 men in five days. Suffered heavy casualties. Rain, cold; Men went without food, etc. Lasted 'til middle January before we stopped them.

I asked if the battle lasted 63 days and he said, "*Yes, but the bulk of it... well, look in the book,*" he said. I had looked it up and it read 16 Dec 1944 to 25 Jan 1945. "*Yeah, that was the length of the Bulge, and the rest of it was when we wiped Germany off.*"

A couple of Decembers ago, Clarence went to the hospital with a dangerous bout of pneumonia. The nurse told him he would not be going home for Christmas and how sorry she was. He told her he was fine with that because he wasn't hungry and he was warm. He could have gone on to say that no one was shooting at him. The next Christmas, as he was lost in his thoughts, I learned he could have also added that he wasn't stacking dead bodies on Christmas Eve.

I remember a Christmas card that would come to 'Comrade and Family' from Sgt. Emil Solecki who lived in New York. He served with Clarence during the battle and we were always told he was a heck of a guy. Sgt. Solecki would write things like "button your buttons, ready exercise" and other familiar orders of days gone by. How sad for Clarence the year the card didn't appear. Actually, we were all very sad. Young or not, we knew why.

When we were kids, you would have never known that Christmas was anything but a grand celebration of family, gifts and merry making. As the years have passed us by, I sit here trying to remember a blank stare, a lost thought, a troubled look in Clarence's eyes as if he were back in time. It either wasn't there or he hid it well. Now that I know better, my guess is, he hid it well.

One definite reminder of the past is at mealtime, specifically breakfast. Clarence uses his spoon to scrape and scrape and scrape (if you ever sat through this ritual, I am not exaggerating about the scraping) his toast crumbs into a pile and eats every last one, until his plate is so clean, you can use it again. As I watched him closely, my thought was that he did this because he was hungry at times when he was a child. One day he caught me watching him and he asked if I knew why he did that and he went on to explain. *"I will never forget the sight of the little German kids digging in the garbage for something to eat. I vowed then to never leave a crumb on my plate for as long as I live."*

"Brother Eddie and I, we met overseas, in England," Clarence once told me. Edmund was in the Air Force and it was his job to move the planes across the channel. All four Mathe brothers were in the service at the same time. At first I thought that this was a unique situation, but of course now I know many other families did, too.

Clarence did not come home with the 106th. When he left the prison camp in Heilbronn, the 106th stayed behind. He had the most stripes and enough points to come home, but for that reason, he was made acting 1st Sergeant. That fact delayed his return home.

On December 11, 1945, he boarded the USS Europa in Southampton, England, destination, New York. After his discharge at Camp Grant in Illinois, he had dreams to fulfill that had been put on hold for way too long.

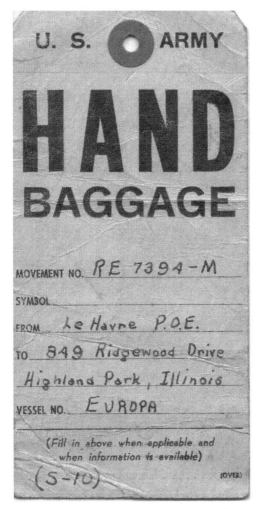

Clarence's baggage tag from Le Havre

I know that I have transported him back in time over and over again with my questions, opening the proverbial can of worms; one that was possibly better left closed. Nevertheless, I was desperate to capture the true story of a young man who had so much influence on me. Thanks for telling me what you could, Dad.

VE Day and VJ Day are the days that should now live in infamy. And when you hear that twenty-one gun salute on November 11th of each year, remember those that fought so valiantly so that you might be free.

I'M COMING TO SEE YOU

Lucille and Grace were no longer working at Badger Ordnance Works in the summer of 1945. They had taken jobs in Wisconsin Dells in a restaurant and Lucille thinks that this is when the idea took hold that the two of them should own a little café.

They went to Chicago on a shopping spree to buy dishes and whatever else they needed for this new endeavor of theirs. Of course due to the war, rationing was still a consideration, but because of the restaurant, they could receive additional amounts of items such as coffee and sugar.

The two sisters were having a grand time while living in the apartment above the restaurant. I can remember looking at this ad for the café and commenting on how late they stayed open at night. Lucille laughed and said, "That didn't last long!"

On most nights, they would close the café and head over to the bowling alley staying up until all hours and each morning they would vow to never, ever do that again. Of course, they always did. In days gone by, when I stayed out late and would say that, I meant it, didn't you?

It was sometime in the month of January in the year of 1946, that Melvin walked into the little café in his small home town. The same small town he had always sworn to leave for good. He is a little more than a month off the boat having just returned from the Pacific. He's happy to be alive and reflects on how his life has changed. How *he* has changed. In three short years, he feels like he has seen it all and more often than not, wished he hadn't. There are things he will try to forget even though he knows he never will.

BE SURE TO EAT

CHRISTMAS DINNER

SPECIAL—Turkey, baked to perfection with all the trimmings.

at the

Friendship Cafe

Friendship

CHICKEN SERVED EVERY SUNDAY

DINNERS — SHORT ORDERS

WE'RE OPEN 7 a.m. 'til midnight daily except Monday night, Saturday night 'til 2 a.m.

Friendship Café ad, Christmas 1945

So many didn't come home and would give anything to be sitting here waiting to enjoy a home-cooked meal. A meal that is about to be delivered to his table by the most beautiful woman he has ever laid eyes on.

As luck would have it, thanks to his friend, Jim Bloomquist, he and the little co-owner of the café had dined and danced the night away just a few days earlier. It was a blind date that neither will ever forget. He couldn't take his eyes off of her and wondered if this could possibly be the end of his wild days.

Lucille talks about their date. "Grace and I were at the restaurant when Mel and Jim picked us up. We went to the Y-Club. That was the happening place at the time. I would assume we danced. I don't know. And then he went to Milwaukee to go to art school. Oh, we kept in touch, writing back and forth.

He came home on the '400' a quite a bit. I guess to see me, but also to see his Dad.

"It has been so many years, I don't always remember where we went or what we did. I do remember going over to the Silver Lake Ballroom in Wautoma, Wisconsin, quite often. We'd ride along with Jack Oppedesen because he played in the Larry Woodbury Band at the time. Mel wouldn't have danced the polka, though. That just wasn't him."

While they were having all of this fun, Clarence had also arrived back in the states and had gone to Illinois to his aunt and uncle's home to see them. They had always been very kind to him when he was younger. After visiting with them, he headed north to find his little brunette.

Lucille says, "Well, I don't know if he wrote me or called that he was coming to Friendship to see me. I said 'if I'm at the apartment that means I would be waiting for him. Then I said if I'm not at the apartment that means I would go with Mel. Well, I guess I wasn't there."

Clarence's heart was broken and he found his sister and a couple of his old buddies and they proceeded to get drunker than billy goats. This was always one of his favorite sayings. I asked him recently how drunk a billy goat can get and he said, "Pretty darn drunk." And that was said with a pretty darn big smile.

Lucille picks up the story. "I don't remember just when we sold the restaurant, but then we had the little dress shop next door. Grace and I lived in the small apartment upstairs during that time. I think we paid about $800 for the building and eventually sold it for about $2,000.

"We didn't make it in the dress shop but we had fun wearing the dresses we had. When we sold, Picus, from the old department store across the street, bought the rest of them from us."

Even though Mel was not 'the country' as she liked to say, he was always going to write this western story...he liked going to the movies. And he was definitely dressed up when they went.

All of this time when Melvin would come out to the Mikoda farm on Sundays for dinner, he was of course *always* dressed in a suit and tie and Lucille's Dad *always* had on his bib overalls.

I wish I had been a little mouse in the corner during this time. Grandpa Roger was such a softie with such a gruff voice. But he must have totally approved of this young man courting his youngest daughter, because when Melvin died, Roger cried. And, I might add that one of the stories Melvin wrote was a western.

LOHENGRINS MARCH

When Grace married John Trzesniak in June of 1947, Lucille was her maid of honor. Her dress was stunning and she looked radiantly beautiful. When she was walking up the aisle at church, Mel told her afterward that he wanted to tell them to stop and "make it two." And yet it was more than a year later before they were married. Melvin must have still been set on getting a little nest egg put away as he always told his Dad he would before settling down. Either that, or his constant declaration of being a confirmed bachelor, still got the best of him. When they finally decided it was time, I wondered how they set the date.

Lucille says, "Well, I guess we just kind of took it for granted that we were going to get married, I don't know. And we knew it was going to be in the fall, but it wasn't going to be September 27th because that was the day his mother died. So then it was a week later on October 2nd."

I asked what her parents thought of them getting married.

"I don't know, I guess it must have been okay," Lucille says. "The only thing I remember is the morning I was going to get married, Dad and Mom and I were having breakfast, and Dad said, "Well this is the last time you're going to eat breakfast as Lucille Mikoda.

"He wasn't sad. It's just that in those days, people didn't show much emotion one way or another. You never hugged anybody or told them that you loved them or anything. It was a sissy thing, I think."

In one of Melvin's late 1943 letters to his Dad, he had commented on his cousin Natalie deciding to change religions (to Catholic) in order to get married. According to him, "didn't that beat all!" Well, guess what?!

Lucille, maid of honor for Grace and John

Lucille is quite amused as she says, "He should talk! He had to go to classes with Father Brudermann before we could get married at St. Josephs. I had to laugh, because Mel would ask Father all of these complex questions about what he was trying to tell him. And of course Father didn't always have the answers so his response eventually was just to tell him that that is where your faith comes in!"

Lucille and Melvin's wedding picture

The marriage did take place, at St. Josephs, and the Rev. L. Brudermann did officiate. There was quite a write up in the local paper which everyone had forgotten about until I came across it on microfilm at the library one day. I found it enchanting!

Entering the church to the strains of Lohengrin's wedding march, the bride looked lovely in her trim tailored suit of light gray wool gabardine. Her accessories were black with a touch of rhinestone and she wore a rhinestone choker, a gift of the groom. Her shoulder corsage was of red roses and white lilies of the valley.....

After the reception and having received many beautiful and useful gifts (per the article), they moved to Milwaukee where Mel was employed and the letters to his father continued. Only now he wrote about the two of them.

Sun P.M.

Dear Dad -

Lucy and I are just sitting around the kitchen & listening to the radio with nowhere to go & nothing to do so I figured it was as good a time as any to drop a line.

If you're coming down next Sun, let us know. But don't come down the 30th, at least to see us, as we'll be coming home for Lu's birthday - (the first.)

How did you like the Packers today? I did, even if I did lose $2.00 on the deal.

The frau is here looking over my shoulder at everything. Now she's snickering. She says to tell you she's going to work Tues. at Scheusters here on the south side.

Sunday seems so short. Here it is almost time to hit the sack & it seems like I just got up.

I'll probably write again before the 30th so be good & write us - Love Lu & Mel xx

Regardless of where he was, he wrote to his father. Thank heavens for that or I wouldn't have known what I now do about Melvin. No one was keeping anything from me, it was just a part of the past that we didn't talk about. And I never asked. Their never seemed to be a reason to dredge up the emptiness we always felt when he was mentioned.

ONE OF EACH

Shortly after that letter, Melvin took a job in Waco, Texas. They were still newlyweds so the first chance Lucille had to join him, she did. Her Uncle Leo and his family were going by train to California, so Lucille rode along as far as Fort Worth where she was reunited with her new husband. In her letters to her parents, she tells them how cold it was when they left Fort Worth on their way back to the Midwest sometime later and she wondered if Grace had told them that she might be making them grandparents.

At least she thought so. She was very anxious to know for sure because she didn't feel any different. Either she wasn't pregnant or she was just tough was her thinking.

She has always been tough, but she was also pregnant and it wasn't long after Mark was born that she was expecting again. Manley's smile grew, Melvin was a little apprehensive and Lucille was *not* thrilled. She was not ready for another baby so soon. They were living in Indiana where Mel was working and shortly after Mark's first birthday, the plan was to move to Texas again. The doctor in Indiana had given them a referral there to continue with her care. But at some point, the decision was made that Lucille would go back to Wisconsin and stay with her folks for the time being.

In one of our quiet moments together, she had a few things to say about being pregnant again so soon. When we had this conversation, it was because I was pretty much in her shoes some years back. I had just had a baby and was expecting again. But she told me she didn't know how she could have ever been unhappy about it once she looked at my tiny little face. As a matter of fact, recently, we were looking at a scrapbook album I had made for her. There I was, six weeks old smiling at her from the pages that were of me. She said I was the cutest baby she had ever seen. She thought that then and said she still thinks so now.

I had arrived on November 11, 1950. I came into this world in the little brick building across from the old Catholic Church on Main Street Adams, Wisconsin, for the whopping cost of $103.60. I still have the receipt and the canceled check.

Melvin was so proud of the fact that they had proven that they could make 'one of each.' Since he was working out of town at the time, Grace sent him a telegram announcing my arrival. And he couldn't wait to see me. He wrote to Mom that I must be a sweet little honey girl and so small next to bull-moose Markey.

Cousin Natalie told me that when the four of us would visit their Gram Newkirk, they couldn't get over how Melvin would change diapers and would just glory in taking care of me. Strange word to describe how he took to being a father, but I love the fact that he did. Most men back then thought it was all women's work. Way to go Mel!

TAPS

"I told you what happened that November day so many years ago. But I didn't tell you about that day." Those were Mom's words to me just out of the blue one day not long ago.

Work wasn't always the easiest to find, especially in a small town and yet Melvin didn't want to be so far away anymore. In his March 1951 birthday card to his father, he wrote that he hoped the weather would turn warmer so that Richardson would be opening up. Richardson was a painting company out of Baraboo, Wisconsin.

Lucille reflects on this time. "Even when we lived in town of course there wasn't much for jobs. He didn't like factory work. When he first came home from the war, he worked for Roberts' Brothers Garage as a bookkeeper. And then when they did the clearing of the land for the dam, he was the bookkeeper then, too. He was good at that. But all of that stuff never paid a doodlydarn. So when Richardson did open up, he went. If I'd have been smart, I'd have told him to get a different job and not chase all over. He was so smart, he could have done anything."

In November of 1951, a crew of fifteen men were working in Winona, Minnesota. We were staying in the little mobile home we owned and had parked by the farm on 'Z' by Grandma and Grandpa. Melvin was home for the weekend.

The picture of the four of us taken in the living room at the old farm on my first birthday is the last picture of us together.

Mom holding me and Melvin is holding Mark, November 11, 1951

I'm one of those people who has to make a conscious effort not to give in to heartbreak. As I tell this part of the story, my efforts are failing miserably. We were the perfect little family. I think about Mom now and how it was almost sixty years before she really talked about it. Or was it sixty years before she knew I was ready to listen. Maybe a little of both. This is when she said that she told me what happened that day, nothing more about that day. Until now.

Mom is staring off into the distance as she tells me, "I remember a man coming to the farm and my Dad leaving with him. A short while later, when they returned, Manley was with them. I knew. Oh, I knew then he wasn't coming back. I felt like my life was over."

In all of the sixty plus years since, Mom had never said anything like that to me. As she spoke softly of that day, we shared a deep sadness for what might have been, both knowing that what-if's serve no purpose.

His job as a steeple jack paid very well, but it cost him his life. When the work was complete, he was assigned to take the rigging down. While he was at the top, he slipped from the bosun's chair and fell 128 feet. A terrible way to make the front page of the paper with a picture of the building and arrows drawn showing your descent. The men inside the building thought there had been an explosion on the roof and ran to find the cause.

The sounds of him moaning made it an easy discovery. He was still alive, but thankfully not for long. I can no longer read the article in the Winona Herald. It just plain hurts.

Lucille told me she saw her Dad cry twice in her life, and Mel's death was one of those times. I have never asked what Grandpa Manley must have been like when they brought him back to the farm that day. I don't think I ever will. I doubt Mom could have seen past her agony to witness his.

Grace and John were living in Chicago when Lucille sent her this telegram. To this day, Grace gets very choked up as she tells of what a terrible time this was for everyone.

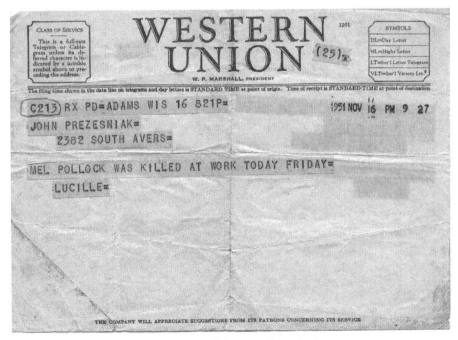

The telegram Lucille sent to her sister Grace

Melvin's cousin Natalie was at his funeral and voiced her thoughts about that day. She told me that when they played taps at the cemetery, "your mother just sank." At the age of eighty-eight, she remembered that so vividly. As they said their good-byes at his grave side, there was a beautiful sunset and she heard someone make the comment that Melvin must be at peace. I find no peace in what happened. There have been well over 22,000 sunsets since then, and he has missed them all.

After the service, Bob Dunham, Melvin's best friend approached Lucille and was so distraught he couldn't speak. He walked away and that was the last she ever saw of him. And another friend of his, Ralph Kenyon, gave her a ten dollar bill and told her to go buy a hat. Hats always made women feel better. When I heard that story, I was speechless. His intentions were good, but how strange. However, I doubt he would have known what else to say during such sorrow. And we each handle life or in this case, death, differently.

Christmas was only a few weeks later. Once again, there is a picture taken in the living room at the old farm. Only this time, there are only three of us. Lucille's face reflects her pain and yet her shoulders are straight as they bear the weight of her world.

Mark and I with Mom at Christmas

As with any loss, life continues and the survivors must go on. And Mom had Mark and I to think of now. We of course had no clue as to what was wrong. I honestly remember nothing. Not at the age of one. Is that good or bad? Sometimes I would give anything to at least say I remember his face and his smile. As the years have passed, that vision may have faded away, too.

Eventually, Mom purchased a little house on Linden Street. We lived there for a few years and when I look at the pictures of those times now, the smiles slowly returned. At least for Mark and I. What a blessing childhood is.

Along with the healing came another return of sorts.

LIFE GOES ON

On Memorial Day, 1952, there is a dance at the Dellwood Pavilion. Lucille hadn't left the house since the funeral so Grace and John convince her that she should get out and accompany them to the shindig. She finally agrees and imagine who she runs into.

Talk about full circle. That is where Lucille, Clarence and friends had spent her sixteenth birthday popping the champagne cork with their buddy Harold. So much had happened in their lives in the mere six years since she stood him up that day at the apartment. And now they are together once more. They started seeing each other occasionally and the rest is history.

Clarence told me recently that he was scared to death of her father. I remember Grandpa Roger well and his bark was worse than his bite. However, I also feel that a slight fear of your elders is a sign of respect. And with respect foremost in his mind, three years after they were reacquainted, Clarence asked him for her hand in marriage. He was told, "If you take care of those kids, yes. But only if you take care of those kids." As he tells this story so many years later, I am once again dealing with crocodile tears. As he looks up at me, he says, "I hope I have done that, honey. I hope I have."

They drove to Dubuque, Iowa, on Thanksgiving Day and somehow Clarence managed to find someone to marry them. On a holiday. Imagine that. The pictures from a reception held later shows everyone having a good time dancing while Mark and I assist with the cake cutting.

Clarence and Lucille celebrating

Clarence repeatedly has said that I was always so sad looking and that he just wanted to make me smile. I have pictures of those times and everyone is smiling again. Including me.

We continued to live in the house on Linden Street next to the old Quonset hut that Grandma Button lived in. I loved that name. I was so excited to later learn that her last name really was Button.

Clarence was working in Illinois and coming home on weekends. Making a living in small town America where we were was still not easy. And our family was growing. I had two sisters now.

Grace and John had moved back up from Chicago by then and Grace usually stopped in when she was in town. She tried calling first on this particular day, but Lucille never answered the phone. She couldn't. The house was full of carbon monoxide and it wouldn't have been long for any of us. We were starting to pass out. Grace saved us and Clarence was crazed. End of Linden Street for us.

He bought forty acres out in the country and built us a mansion. At least that's how I looked at it. I had my own room and it was painted pink. I loved that house and used to dream that I lived there when I got older.

Once someone couldn't pay Clarence for some work he had done, so he took horses in trade. They ate too much and were a lot of work so they didn't last long, but talk about fun while we had them. And an old mobile home showed up one day. Another barter I would imagine. What a play house that made! I remember it like it was yesterday. My sisters and I played with paper dolls and Barbie dolls in there. I don't think we spent the night in it, though. Heebee-jeebees ya' know.

Another mansion memory was growing pickles. I can't imagine how this came about. Maybe Gram Mikoda, the garden guru, was the instigator. We picked them every other day which must have been quite a chore, but I don't remember any of us grumbling too much. I'm sure we did at times, but it was extra money, especially for the small ones, and we got to ride to the pickle factory in Dellwood with Lucille at the wheel. On one of our trips, there was a car stalled on Bruce's bridge and the brakes on our old Nash Rambler decided to fail. We had pickles all over the place. The Nash had push-button shifting which, to this day, I still think is unique. What was really cool is that Lucille didn't even have a license. She lost her purse many years before and never bothered having her license replaced. Hilarious don't you think? And if there are any officers of the law from back then reading this, if you ever stopped her (like the one time because the muffler was loud), you should have asked her for her license and not how the kids were doing. Oops! Too late!

We actually had a stage in the lower level of the house. Almost the entire front wall of the family room was a fireplace with a ledge. That was where we held our pageants. The talent competition ranged from singing to dancing to acting. Such fun on a narrow piece of concrete.

There were so many great things about being a kid. Everything was fun. Birthdays were always the best. And Christmas? What can I say. We always celebrated on Christmas Eve and anyone and everyone seemed to be at our house. The presents were piled high under the tree and Santa never disappointed. We had a small aluminum tree in the upstairs living room that we would decorate with just one color of ornaments, but the fresh cut tree in the family room down by the fireplace was the big deal. It was always so beautiful. I don't remember one time that we didn't get what we had asked for. I know now as a parent that it wasn't always an easy task to make that happen.

Since Melvin's memory was always with us, each year, Grandpa Manley would be our very special guest. He, too, was always dressed to the nines. Like father, like son. We'd have a huge dinner and after the dishes were done, we would open all of those gifts. Then while still dressed in our festive attire, we would head into town to attend midnight mass. Manley would climb into the front seat next to Lucille for the ride home. Yes, she would always drive. Prior to arriving at St. Joseph's, we would leave him at the doorstep of the old hotel where he had rented a room so many years before. Now as I look back, he was always a little more forlorn than the year before. If he had any religious affiliation, I wouldn't know because I never asked. Shame on me.

What I wouldn't give to have my time with him again. If I were the person then that I am now, I would have moved heaven and earth to pull him out of his solitude. When he was in the hospital before he passed away in May of 1970, he asked me what the weather was like. Because it was raining and I now considered myself an adult, I told him it was rather 'pissy.' He was so surprised he actually smiled. Such a good guy he was.

He lived almost nineteen years longer than his son. And in those nineteen years, he had to have wondered many times what life would have been like if Melvin hadn't fallen that day. My mind wanders that same path quite often and the conclusion remains the same. We will never know.

At some point, Lucille and Clarence had purchased the old farmhouse that she was born in. When they moved some of their belongings there, the boxes containing Melvin's letters, etc. were among the things being stored, and unfortunately missed when the house was sold to Clarence's brother. Thankfully his grandchildren found the boxes in later years and thought to ask who they might belong to. The name Pollock was not something they knew.

Eventually the mansion was sold and we moved down across from Castle Rock Park. A new house was built next to our motel. In the late 60's, cabins were moved from Wisconsin Dells and the Hiawatha Resort came to life. So many people stayed there over the course of thirty-five years and the stories that Lucille could tell! We always wanted her to write a book titled "The Last Resort." She met a lot of interesting people, that's for sure.

THE GOLDEN YEARS

Someone once said, "Before you know, the future is the past." I think I have firmly established that fact. The resort was sold and another new home was built. This will no doubt be the last home that Lucille and Clarence will share. But after fifty-eight years of marriage, they have no complaints. They are still together.

As I have been writing this story, I have observed my parents as they are today. Sometimes it's hard to picture them as they once were. They are no longer vibrant and only move with the ability that time and age allows. Their walkers are parked by each of their chairs for the added security that has become necessary.

I'm not sure at what age the golden years begin, but if this is it, well, it just isn't. They will both tell you that life has been good, they have had a lot of fun, but these days, such is not the case.

Each morning, Mom shuffles into the kitchen and starts the coffee brewing. She'll then sit at the table and wait for Dad to make his appearance. After he sits a minute and catches his breath, he reaches for her hand and says, "love you, a bushel and a peck and a hug around the neck." Mom's response? "Okay." Every morning.

When she knows the coffee has stopped dripping and is safe to pour, she gets up, and holding onto the counter all the while, she pours the brown liquid adding just the right amount of half and half to each cup and delivers the 'wake up' beverage to each place mat. The same plastic peach placemats that have been there forever.

And each night after they are finally ready for bed, Dad with the last of the inhalers for the day, will thank her for everything she always does for him and that he will see her in the morning...God willing.

Not long ago, I heard Mom tell someone that she used to be afraid of dying; now she says she is afraid of living. So many times when I look at them, I can see in their eyes that it just isn't worth it some days. I know how tired you both are.

When it's time, I know that I will fall apart. There will be such an unbearable emptiness at first, but as all of the memories come flooding in, that emptiness will fill with our precious moments and make me whole once more.

It will take a little time, but I promise, not too long. And then, yes, I will bow my head, once again, in honor and in prayer for always having been so lucky to have had the two of them for my Mom and my Dad.

THE FINAL LETTERS

One day can change your life forever. One moment can do the same.

My life has taken on a direction these past few years that I never would have envisioned and what a roller coaster ride it has been. I am very thankful to have been given the chance to learn more about the days that have gone by and possibly be more in tune to the ones ahead.

Someday, my newfound WWII memorabilia will be on display for all to see. The time and place has yet to be determined. For now, I plan to savor the history that I had ignored for so long and now consume with a ferocity that even I cannot explain.

The stories of the Pacific outnumber the stories of Europe, but Melvin was more of a writer than Clarence was a talker. It is what it is. What I know for certain is that my emotions have run the gamut of a lifetime since this all began.

Life is a crazy proposition if you ask me. We can set our own course, try to veer in the right direction and hope for the best. But in the end, or should I say when the end comes, the choice won't be ours.

While you are in control, you must live life to the fullest, become whatever it is you want to be, and be as happy as you can for as long as you can.

It was letters that began the story. Appropriately, letters will end the story. I have written to each of my parents, no longer using first names.

Dear Dad,

How do you say good bye when you have never said hello? I think of you so often, but never so much as these last few years. All that I have of you is what is on paper and a few brief memories from the minds of those who knew you.

I remember the day the remnants of your life were given to me. I remember my first glance into the past. And I remember the contents of the boxes bringing me to my knees in tears. But I don't remember you.

The letters you wrote to Grandpa were a blessing to be cherished forever. Thankfully they came to me at a time in my life when I was old enough to appreciate what I had and yet young enough to savor the contents for the balance of my years.

As I sit here trying to put my thoughts and my feelings into words, the tears run down my now aging cheeks. Gently at first, but soon my vision is completely blurred. I can no longer ease my unease where you are concerned. I am in mourning.

Some would say I was cheated when you died. But I refused to ever use it as an excuse for not living life to the fullest. My loss was never going to guide my days. I have always had too much I needed or wanted to do to feel sorry for myself. I only regret that you never experienced all of the things I have.

Your cousin Natalie said I am a lot like you. That comment made me feel like you were truly a part of me all along. I was and am, very blessed.

I have struggled with the Catholic faith now for years as I've grown older. But the one thing I am convinced of, is that there is a heaven and one day you and I will be reunited. Mom wonders if we will know each other, yet I harbor no doubts. No matter what form we are in, we will know. I believe this. I have to believe this. It has been my only comforting thought all of my life where you are concerned. Father Bruderman would say that this is where my faith comes in.

I could speculate all day long how different things might have been had you lived. But there is no reason to do so. It is what it is and that's that. Mom would tell you that, you know.

We both wonder if you would have eventually settled for a different profession and stayed home with us. I'm sure of it. The wandering would get old and the love you held in your heart for us would have prevailed.

I'll be seeing you, Dad. But if it's okay, none too soon. I'm just not finished here yet.

All for now, Pop.

Love to the best Dad of all,

From your best and favorite daughter, Marcia xxxooo

Dear Mom,

I think you know how much you mean to me. We have been so fortunate to have the relationship that we do and have had the chance to enjoy every moment we could. I thank God every day for you. You mean the world to me.

There isn't anything I wouldn't do for you. These days it's hard for you to leave the house. There was a time when you did humor me on occasion and accompany me to different events. And you always had fun once you were there.

The day I dragged you over to the Senior Center to listen to the music session was one such day. All the while you were getting ready you were shooting mild daggers at me. Finally you said, "You are the only one I would do this for!" Remember, I laughed and said, "I know that, Mom." But you went and you tapped your toes the whole time.

And I will never forget when I took you to see Ray Price. I vividly remember that day and how you sat through the concert in awe as you silently sang along with all of the old songs. What a beautiful memory we made. Afterwards, you sent a note to thank me for taking time from my busy life to make an eighty-year old lady so happy. You hoped when I was that age, someone would do something just as nice for me. I hope so, too, Mom. I hope to be as worthy as you so that someone will want to.

You have made a lasting impression on me and everyone who knows you. Thank you for being you.

I love you Mom.

Dear Dad,

I begin with simple words. I love you Dad. And you are my Dad. Thanks for marrying us on that November day in 1954.

You taught us to look forward with eager enthusiasm and to look back with grateful hearts. You had a tough childhood and yet I do not remember a time while growing up that you ever felt sorry for yourself.

Instead, you instilled in us a sense of family, a good work ethic and a deep appreciation for life. I repeat your wise mantra quite often. If you have your health, you have everything. How true.

When Mom's health, and yours, started to fail, it was another chapter in our lives that we couldn't change. However, the three of us formed a bond through this time that I will cherish the rest of my days.

Everything we already knew about life took on a deeper meaning. Each day became more precious. We learned to cry without restrictions and laugh without restraint.

We have survived it all, together. As a family. As it should be. I thank you for who you are, and the impact you have made on my life. You are a good man.

Love, Your Daughter